THE FOCAL EASY GUIDE TO

FINAL CUT PRO X

THE FOCAL EASY GUIDE TO

FINAL CUT PRO X

Second Edition

RICK YOUNG

Focal Press
Taylor & Francis Group

NEW YORK AND LONDON

Technical Editor: Ken Stone
Proof Reader: Fiona Lewis

First published 2013 by Focal Press

This edition published 2015
by Focal Press
70 Blanchard Road, Suite 402, Burlington, MA 01803

and by Focal Press
2 Park Square, Milton Park, Abingdon, Oxon OX14 4RN

Focal Press is an imprint of the Taylor & Francis Group, an informa business

Notices
Knowledge and best practice in this field are constantly changing. As new research
and experience broaden our understanding, changes in research methods,
professional practices, or medical treatment may become necessary.

Practitioners and researchers must always rely on their own experience and
knowledge in evaluating and using any information, methods, compounds, or
experiments described herein. In using such information or methods they should be
mindful of their own safety and the safety of others, including parties for whom they
have a professional responsibility.

Product or corporate names may be trademarks or registered trademarks, and are
used only for identification and explanation without intent to infringe.

Library of Congress Cataloging in Publication Data
Young, Rick, 1967–
   The Focal easy guide to Final cut pro X/Rick Young.—Second edition.
   pages cm
   1. Final cut (Electronic resource) 2. Digital video—Editing—Data
   processing. 3. Video tapes—Editing—Data processing. I. Title. II.
   Title: Easy guide to Final cut pro X.
   TR899.Y692 2015
   777′.9—dc23
   2014021957

ISBN: 978–1-138–78553–3 (pbk)
ISBN: 978–1-315–76775–8 (ebk)

Typeset in Avenir
by Florence Production Ltd, Stoodleigh, Devon, UK

Printed and bound in the United States of America by Sheridan Books, Inc. (a Sheridan Group Company).

Thank you:

Fiona
Ellen
Druman
Ken Stone
Matt Davis
Alex Gollner
Dennis at Focal
Elizabeth Jolley (for the inspiration)

Download footage to edit with

As a purchaser of The Focal Easy Guide to Final Cut Pro X (second edition) you are entitled to download footage to edit with. This can be used as you work through each of the tutorials in the book, or separate from the book where you can experiment, cut projects, and get to know Final Cut Pro X by working with it.

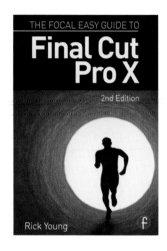

The footage is copyright, so do not distribute or use this in works other than for the purposes of learning Final Cut Pro X. If you need volume licensing for teaching purposes get in touch. We are happy to help!

Enjoy working with the footage which has been transcoded to ProRes Proxy. This will work well with any Mac running Final Cut Pro X and will use a modest amount of hard drive space.

Simply download the footage and import this into Final Cut Pro X. You will then be ready to edit!

To download go to:
www.focalpress.com/9781138785533

Contents

Editing 71

Audio 153

Effects 181

Share and Archive 251

Introduction

It's been a turbulent few years in the editing world and it is only now that the turmoil of recent times is beginning to subside.

When Final Cut Pro X was released it was controversial, it was a radical departure from what had gone before, and even though it showed huge promise that promise was to be realized later, further down the road. The initial release was not regarded by many as a full release, more like a working beta with plenty of bugs to be ironed out

That new day has now arrived—at the time of writing, we are 3 years into the development of Final Cut Pro X, and this editing application has proven itself to be reliable and well-capable for serious professional use.

The application is stable and performs well on a suitably specced machine. You don't need a top of the line Mac to run Final Cut Pro X, though plenty of RAM, fast drives or SSDs do make a big difference.

For old school editors the transition can be difficult while the new concepts are learned. The basics are the same, however, there are different ways of working particularly when it comes to dealing with the database which sits at the heart of this edit system.

For those new to editing, recognize that you are working with tools which are far more sophisticated than the upright or flatbed film editors of yesterday that so many of the great movies were cut with. You can do anything with Final Cut Pro X—from a 30 second commercial to a feature film. The purpose of this book is to open your mind to the possibilities that Final Cut Pro X offers and show you the technical processes step-by-step, so you understand the key functionality on offer. Unless you know what the tool can do you can't use it properly.

I edit with Final Cut Pro X daily and weekly for paying clients. This is my post-production tool. Some say "learn all the editors out there" I say "learn one which works for you." And for me it is Final Cut Pro X which works for me. This is exceptionally quick for organizing and cataloguing footage, compiling an edit and fine-tuning the edit, and then, of course, outputting the material.

You need to know the essentials and it is these which this book will teach you. If you're just beginning with Final Cut Pro X this is a fantastic time to dive in deep with the software which is now full-featured and ready to cut at whatever level you need. The tool is good now go make it work for you.

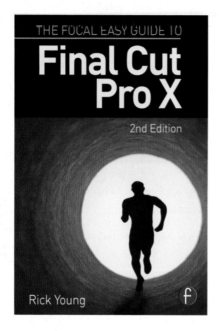

"Go fly with this software, it's got wings."

Rick Young
Harrogate UK
February 2014

WWW.FOCALPRESS.COM/9781138785533

DOWNLOAD COMPLIMENTARY FOOTAGE TO EDIT WITH.

General Editing Playback Import Destinations

SYSTEM SETUP

A Word about Preferences

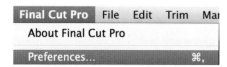

Setting up Preferences is not the most exciting place to start, however, it can save you a lot of hassle later on by getting it right from the beginning.

The Preferences in Final Cut Pro X are relatively sparse compared to the myriad of choices offered in some editing programs.

There are five separate panes:

General, Editing, Playback, Import and Destinations. The most important of these for setting up your system are Editing, Playback and Import.

Editing Preferences

For the most part, the Editing Preferences can be left at their defaults. I suggest making sure the two following options are checked: Show Detailed Trimming Feedback and Position Playhead after Edit Operation.

Timeline: ☑ Show detailed trimming feedback
☑ Position playhead after edit operation

To active Detailed Trimming Feedback means when using the Trim mode while editing, the feedback display will be that of two windows: one showing the outgoing clip and the other showing the incoming clip. You can precisely fine-tune edits by watching the dual display. This functionality will be useful once we begin the editing process.

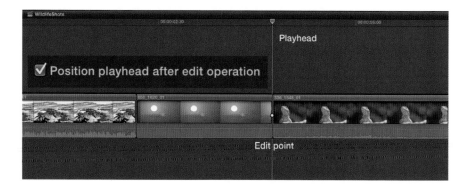

Selecting Position Playhead after Edit Operation means that each time you perform an edit, then what is known as the Playhead—the point which defines where you are in the Timeline, will be left in position immediately after where the edit has taken place.

Playback Preferences

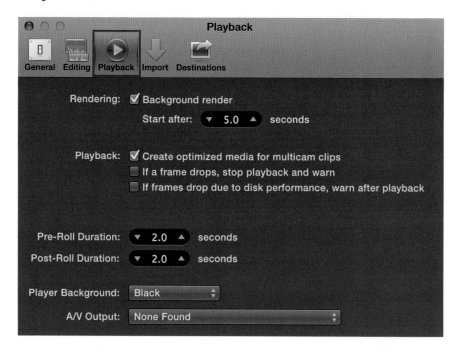

As with the Editing Preferences, most of the Playback Preferences can be left at the default settings; however, it is worth understanding the key options in front of you as what you choose will affect the performance of your system. We will work our way down from the top.

Background Render

Choose whether you wish to have Background Rendering switched on or off.

Rendering: ☑ Background render

With Background Rendering switched on this means that when you are not working, the computer will render the frames of your movie in full pristine quality for you to view. If you leave Background Rendering switched on, after the defined time, then the computer will kick in and render any media in the Timeline which needs to be processed.

It may be that you don't want the computer to do the rendering while you are working, in which case switch

☐ Background render

Background Render off. Render files consume hard drive space, and while these can be easily deleted, there are times when one may wish to avoid rendering until you are ready.

My preference is to leave Background Rendering switched off. I like to define when rendering takes place and do not wish to generate render files until I need content rendered in the Timeline.

Playback: ☑ Create optimized media for multicam clips

If you plan on working with Multicam clips in your work then you may wish to check the Create optimized media for multicam clips. This means if the footage is difficult for Final Cut Pro X to work then the footage will be converted to another format (ProRes) which Final Cut Pro X can easily work with. Beware that the conversion process can take some time.

I do work with Multicam frequently. I choose to leave this option unchecked. I would rather manually convert my footage, if needed. Otherwise you may find a great deal of hard drive consumed due to the conversion process. However, if you are just starting out I suggest leaving this option checked. You can always go back into Preferences and switch this off if you choose.

The rest of the Playback Preferences you can leave at the defaults. Note the AV Output if you are working with external monitoring.

A/V Output: None Found

Import Preferences

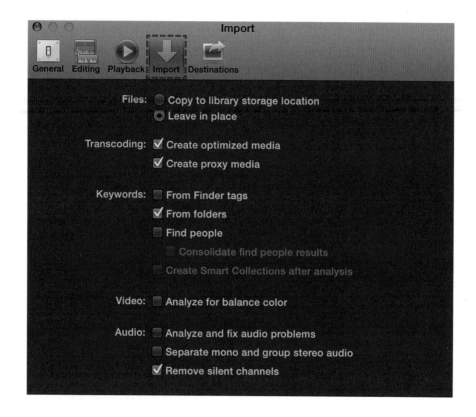

Several of the Import Preferences are crucial to defining how you work with Final Cut Pro X. The first option is very important: Copy to Library Storage Location or Leave in Place. If you leave this option checked, then every media file used in the project will be copied into an area known as the Library. A Library is stored on hard drive, wherever you define, and you have a choice of whether to include all of your media internal, within the Library, or external, which means elsewhere on hard drive wherever you define.

If you choose to Copy files to Library Storage Location this is 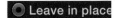 referred to as a Managed Library. Effectively you are handing control to Final Cut Pro X to take care of managing your media for you. You need to be careful defining where you store the Library, on hard drive, as all your media will then be copied into the Library. You therefore need to make sure you store the Library on a hard drive with plenty of room to store the media (avoid using your boot drive if possible). Effectively, using Copy to Library Storage Location means that you are leaving it to Final Cut Pro X to do all the media management for you (Note: when importing camera originals from media card these files will need to be imported to the Library Storage Location, unless you plan on leaving the media card online while editing!)

The downside to choosing Copy to Library Storage Location is that you will consume a lot of hard drive space as the media will exist in its original location and also within the Library you are working with. While you could remove the original files, once copied, this is risky, in case something goes astray.

Rather than allow Final Cut Pro X to copy all the media to the Library Storage Location, the alternative is to choose Leave in Place. This applies when importing media which already exists on hard drive. These media files will then remain on hard drive in the location where you have defined, and Final Cut Pro X will then reference to these files. This means the files are not copied from one location to another location - rather they remain wherever you have chosen to store them.

As the name implies, Leave in Place means Final Cut Pro X works with the files wherever you have chosen to store them on hard drive.

Therefore, when working with a Library which you choose to manage yourself, using Leave files in place, as opposed to a Managed Library, where Final Cut Pro X copies the files into the Library, it is important to be aware that if the original media is moved or deleted, then your project will no longer work. You can cause irreparable damage. Provided you are careful and go to the effort of putting the media in a folder, somewhere safe, then you should have no trouble.

You therefore need to define whether you wish to work with a Managed Library or if you wish to manually decide where your media will be stored. The fact is, even when you choose to Leave in place, much of the time some of the media will end up being copied to the Library if files need to be Transcoded.

Furthermore, as already mentioned, files imported from memory card or other devices will be copied to the Current Library. It is only media, already stored on hard drive, which does not need transcoding that can be external to the Library.

Note the next choice in the Import Preferences which is Transcoding.

Transcoding: ☑ Create optimized media
☐ Create proxy media

In most cases I leave Create Optimized Media checked. This means any media which Final Cut Pro X decides is difficult to work with, such as AVCHD or H.264, will automatically be transcoded to ProRes on import. If the media can be easily worked with in its current form, then it will be left in its original state. Regardless, when transcoding files Final Cut Pro X always retains the original media for future use, so nothing is lost!

It is important to be aware that if media is transcoded it will be stored within the Library, even if you have chosen to Leave in place. Anytime Final Cut Pro X needs to transcode, generate media or render files, then these files will be stored within the Library. You will get a much better sense of how Libraries work once we get onto organization and editing. For now, just know that the Library is the place where everything is stored for the editing process, be it media files, render files, graphics, audio or anything else—with the proviso being that external media files will be referenced to, if you select Leave files in place, providing they do not need to be transcoded.

◉ Leave in place

You don't need to leave Create optimized media checked—however, it is advisable to do so. Final Cut Pro X is pretty good at determining if media needs to be transcoded for fluid playback and trouble-free editing. Regardless, you can choose to work with this option unchecked—which some do, as optimizing media, when required, will take time and use up hard drive space. You can always choose to optimize media, at a later time, after Import.

You can also choose to work with Proxy media.

Working with Proxy media provides the ability to switch between full-resolution media and low-resolution ProRes Proxy files. For this to take place, the media must be transcoded. By leaving the option Create Proxy Media checked on import, the low-resolution Proxy files will automatically be generated.

☑ Create proxy media

I tend to leave this option switched off. Working with smaller proxy files will undeniably provide for better performance, the expense is that these files need to be generated, which takes up time, system resources, and hard drive space.

While in general I leave the Create Proxy Media option switched off, if you find your system is choking or stuttering whilst playing or outputting video, or if you have plenty of time and wish to experiment, then let Final Cut Pro X build the Proxies and you will get a feel for the result. Because the Proxies run at a low data rate, rendering will be quicker and the speed of the system will feel more responsive and fine tuned. You can then, at any point switch between the low resolution Proxy files or full resolution camera original media or transcoded media.

Like optimized media you can choose to generate Proxy files later. This does not need to be done on import. This will be covered later in the editing chapter.

I always leave the option checked—Keywords: From folders. The importance of Keyword Collections will become clear when we begin editing and filing media. For this moment, be aware that naming the folder on hard drive before you import, will result in the name of that folder being applied to the collection of the clips in what is known as a Keyword Collection.

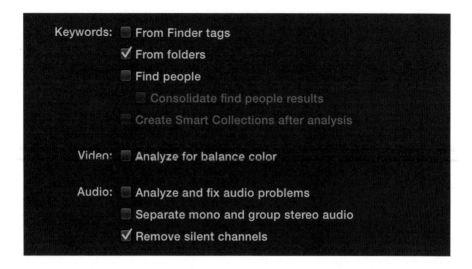

The other options in Import Preferences I usually leave switched off. For my editing, I do not want the computer to analyze my footage for color balance on import or to look for audio problems. These are tasks I would prefer to do manually myself. I do, however, leave the option switched on in the Audio settings to Remove silent channels.

Note: Leaving these options unchecked does not mean you lose the ability to perform these tasks. Each of the processes can be done later during editing.

Note: The two options I haven't covered in Preferences: General and Destinations. Leave these at their defaults.

The Destinations are to do with distribution of your edited movies. Once you have completed the postproduction process, you can choose to output your Project to various formats such as DVD, Blu-ray, as a master file, or to encode to many different formats. This area in Preferences enables you to add several options for distribution output beyond those provided at the defaults.

What Apple gives you with Final Cut Pro X is a complete editing system. Do not underestimate the power of Final Cut Pro X. Compared to the suites of yesterday, this is a tremendously capable editing system with features we couldn't have even dreamed of.

THE INTERFACE

The Three-Window Interface

The interface of Final Cut Pro X is split into three windows: the Browser, the Viewer, and the Timeline.

The Browser is where you access the media with which you build your edited movie. Here, all the Projects, clips, audio files, graphic elements, and music are filed away for you to access, in Filmstrip view or List view.

You can quickly toggle between Filmstrip view and List view by pressing the controls at the bottom of the Browser.

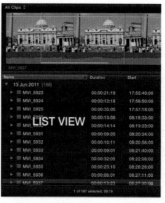

Use the controls to switch between the two views.

The Viewer: this is where you watch the camera original footage when playing clips in the Event Library; or where you view the edited movie by playing back in the Timeline.

Note: By clicking the bottom right of the window you can switch to full screen viewing. Press escape to get out of full screen view.

Timeline: you build your edited movie here. Shots, represented by blocks, are positioned and moved around in relation to other shots, thus enabling the editing process to take place. Clips can be viewed in different ways, audio can be separated from video, and tools can be used to perform different editing tasks.

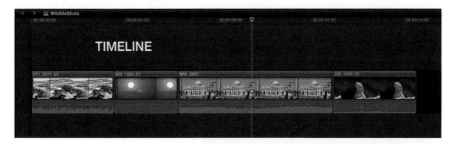

You can switch between different views of the clips in the Timeline by using the Change Clip Appearance Controls (bottom right of the Timeline).

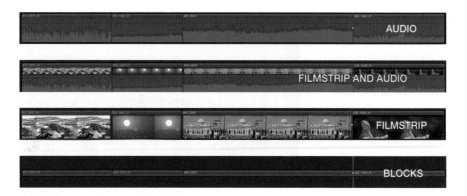

The appearance and size of the video and audio clips can be adjusted as needed. These views can be useful depending on the complexity of the edit and whether you are editing video, audio, or a combination of both.

The Five-Window Interface

The three-window interface can easily be extended to become a five-window interface. Two additional windows are now present: the Inspector and the Effects Browser.

The Inspector is a window you will refer to regularly. Here, parameters can be adjusted relating to the media you are working with in the Timeline or the Browser. You can adjust color correction and audio settings, crop, distort, and position the image, and switch on or off image stabilization.

Three separate tabs  can be accessed for video, audio, and media info.

The shortcut to call up the Inspector is Command + 4 or press the Inspector symbol to the middle far right of the interface.

The Effects Browser provides a gateway to a wide range of sophisticated effects to draw upon. First-class Chroma keying, Luma keying, and a host of customizable and prebuilt options are offered. Everything from blurs to audio distortion can be accessed. Other tabs offer Titles, Transitions, and Generators.

Note: At any time you can return to the simplistic three-window interface by selecting the Window menu at the top of the interface. Scroll down and choose Revert to Original Layout. Most editing work will be done with either the three-window or five-window setup unless you are working with a dual monitor display.

You can also click on the Inspector icon or Effects icon to close these windows.

Working with Dual Viewers

There are times when it can be very useful, for side by side comparison of shots, to work with two Viewers. You can therefore park the Playhead in the Timeline on a shot, and likewise, park the Playhead in the Browser, on a shot—this will display each shot in a separate window. This can be particularly useful for "cutting on action" and also for color correction work.

1 Choose the Window menu at the top of the interface and select show Event Viewer.

Show Event Viewer

2 The Event Viewer will now appear to the left of the main Viewer. Select a clip in the Event Browser and this will be displayed in the Event Viewer as you skim through the footage, whereas the display in the main Viewer will be that of the Timeline.

Work with the Event Viewer when useful, however, I find I switch this off when it isn't needed. It may be comforting for users of other editing software applications, and earlier versions of Final Cut Pro, to see the Event Viewer in place. However, I find it quicker and more efficient to work with a single Viewer which will display either the contents of the Events Browser or Timeline, than two separate windows, except, as mentioned, when comparing shots.

Working with Dual Monitor Displays

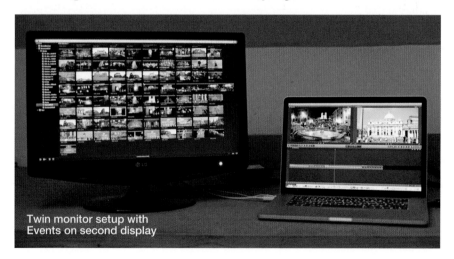

Twin monitor setup with Events on second display

If you want to get serious when editing with Final Cut Pro X, invest in a second monitor. While not essential, it transforms the editing process from a confined, limited work area to an expansive area capable of dealing with large amounts of media.

For a large project, such as a documentary with twenty hours of footage or more, a twin monitor setup would be ideal. Two monitors gives you plenty of space to review and organize footage. While you can certainly work with a single monitor, as on a laptop, two monitors is certainly desirable!

Select the Window menu at the top of the Interface and look at the options towards the bottom. There are two displays when working with dual monitors.

1 Show Events on Second Display: The Events Library is where you organize your footage. When dealing with hundreds or thousands of clips, a large work area is very desirable. A second monitor capable of 1920 x 1080 display is ideal.

**Show Events on Second Display
Show Viewers in the Main Window**

2 Show Viewers on Second Display: Perfect for client viewing and also great for editing. The result is full-screen playback of rushes or edited content, so that you get a much better view than you will with the Viewer or Viewers positioned in the single-window interface.

**Show Events on Second Display
Show Viewers on Second Display**

Show Viewers on Second Display

The Final Cut Pro X interface on a single monitor can get quite crowded; therefore, the advantage of working with dual monitors is that there is room to spread out and be comfortable. The editing experience is not only more enjoyable, you get more done due to the enhanced work area.

Show Events on Second Display

The advantages should be clear. With this dual monitor setup, the Viewer and the Timeline are positioned on one monitor and the Event Library is displayed on the second monitor. Clips can be clearly viewed, labeled, and categorized, in either Filmstrip or List view. I find this display ideal and work with it a lot.

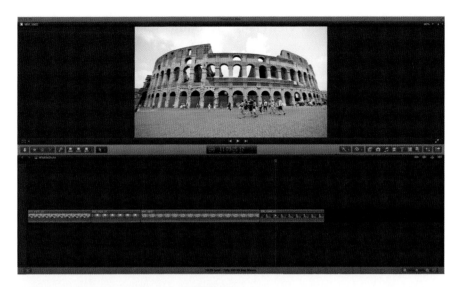

Main monitor shows Viewer and Timeline.

Second monitor shows the Browser and media.

Show Viewers on Second Display

This is for full-screen playback while viewing and editing and provides an effective way to achieve full-screen playback, with the Browser and Timeline positioned on the main display. The large space for the Browser provides for a good-size work area.

Main monitor shows events library and timeline.

Second monitor shows viewer full-screen.

In the examples below you can clearly see the increased screen real estate, when working with two screens.

IMPORTING MEDIA

ame	Start	End	Duration	Content Created	File
■ Clip #93	02:36:55;12	02:39:54;18	00:02:59;04	10 Apr 2014 20:35:41	AV
■ Clip #94	02:39:54;18	02:41:04;20	00:01:10;02	10 Apr 2014 20:38:43	AV
■ Clip #95	02:41:04;20	02:41:07;20	00:00:03;00	10 Apr 2014 20:40:26	AV
■ Clip #96	02:41:07;20	02:41:08;05	00:00:00;15	10 Apr 2014 20:52:09	AV
■ Clip #97	02:41:08;05	02:43:56;09	00:02:48;04	10 Apr 2014 21:07:31	AV
■ Clip #98	02:43:56;09	02:45:26;28	00:01:30;17	10 Apr 2014 21:10:32	AV
■ Clip #99	02:45:26;28	02:46:21;15	00:00:54;15	10 Apr 2014 21:12:28	AV
■ Clip #100	02:46:21;15	02:46:31;00	00:00:09;15	10 Apr 2014 21:14:35	AV
■ Clip #101	02:46:31;00	02:47:00;02	00:00:29;00	10 Apr 2014 21:57:30	AV
■ Clip #102	02:47:00;02	02:47:22;02	00:00:22;00	10 Apr 2014 21:58:15	AV
■ Clip #103	02:47:22;02	02:47:28;17	00:00:06;15	10 Apr 2014 21:58:59	AV
■ Clip #104	02:47:28;17	02:47:37;17	00:00:09;00	10 Apr 2014 21:59:29	AV
■ Clip #105	02:47:37;17	02:47:46;17	00:00:09;00	10 Apr 2014 21:59:46	AV
■ Clip #106	02:47:46;17	02:47:55;17	00:00:09;00	10 Apr 2014 22:06:19	AV
■ Clip #107	02:47:55;17	02:47:59;17	00:00:04;00	10 Apr 2014 22:06:34	AV

Importing Media into Final Cut Pro X

Importing media into Final Cut Pro X is straightforward and trouble-free and this takes place in what is called the Media Import window. More often than not you will import media either (i) directly from the camera or the media card which has recorded the images in-camera (ii) from hard drive.

Often when importing from hard drive the media will already have been converted to a QuickTime format; if so Final Cut Pro X will recognize the files straight away. In cases where files are not recognized, or a camera is not seen by Final Cut Pro X, then you need to either convert the original media to QuickTime (often conversion software is supplied by the camera manufacturer to do this)—or you may need to download a driver or plug-in to enable Final Cut Pro X to see the device or media card and convert the content. Most of the major codecs and formats are supported by Final Cut Pro X. If your camera/media format are not supported you will need to do research online to find the best way to get the files into a form which can be seen and worked with by Final Cut Pro X.

Understanding the Final Cut Pro X file structure

We will cover organization of media in depth in the next chapter. For the moment it is important to understand a few essentials.

When importing media you need to import these files into an Event—an Event is a container, similar to a folder, where all of your media and Project(s) are stored. Media can be video files,

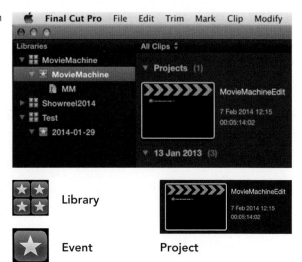

music, still images, graphics and any of the components which you work with in building a movie. The Project refers to your edited Timeline—the place where you have ordered and structured the media to build your movie.

As already described—Events are the place where you store and organize your media; the Project is where the content is edited and structured—all of the Events, Projects and Media live within what is know as the Library. You can and will have many different Libraries to work with. Think of a Library as being the place where everything is stored, the Event being the shelves in the Library—the place where everything is organized—and the Project, represents each of the individual books in a Library—in the case of Final Cut Pro X, each of the movies you have edited.

Therefore, the organizational structure in Final Cut Pro X is hierarchical: the Library is the almighty place where everything to do with your work is filed away. Inside the Library are your Events which contain media and edited Projects. You can have more than one Project stored within a Library and as many Events as you wish.

I would suggest, for ease of knowing where things are, that when working on a specific movie, which could be a documentary, a TV program, a wedding, a feature, an advertisement—whatever it is, create a new Library. You then organize the media within the Library, inside of Events, and then do further fine-detailed organizing of the footage with other tools provided within Final Cut Pro X.

 Showreel 2014

The Library is represented by 4 stars inside of boxes

Create a Library and Importing Media

You need at least one Library open to work within Final Cut Pro X.

1   Choose File—New—Library.

2   Name the Library.

3   Define where the Library is to be stored on hard drive and save it!

The last point is particularly important—defining where the Library is to be stored. This is important for two reasons: (i) You need to know where the Library has been stored so you can find the Library and access this whenever you need to work with it (ii) depending how you have set things up in preferences, the location of the Library will directly affect where your media is stored.

In Preferences, if you choose Copy to Library Storage Location then all media will be self-contained within the Library bundle on hard drive.

If you choose Leave in Place then the Library will reference to the media, wherever this is stored.

Showreel 2014

On the left hand side of the Browser you will visually see the Library you have created in the location where you defined for this to be stored.

Library Bundle as stored on hard drive.

The Library is referred to as a Bundle as it contains the information of your entire project or projects, with media or references to the media. It not just a file on drive—it is a Bundle.

Within the Final Cut Pro X interface the Library you have created appears to the left of the Browser.

Note: By default an Event is created within the Library and this is date stamped. You can click and overtype to rename the Event as you wish.

It is only once you have created the Library that you are ready to begin the Import Process.

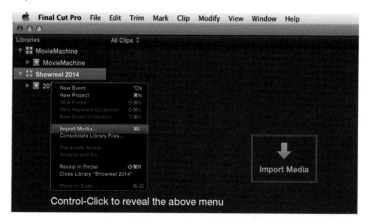

To Import Media either press the large Import Media Button, or Control-click on the Library or Event and select Import Media.

Importing Media

There are several ways to invoke the Import Media command and each of these will take you to the same place, which is the Media Import window.

1   Choose the File—Menu and select Import Media (shortcut Command + i).

2   Control-click either Library or Event and choose Import Media.

3   Press the Import Media button in the Event Browser interface.

4   Far left and middle of the main Final Cut Pro X interface, click the Arrow Button which will open the Media Import window.

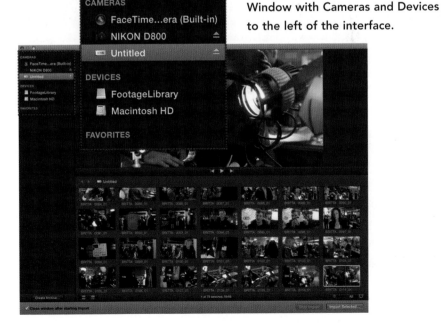

This image shows the Media Window with Cameras and Devices to the left of the interface.

The Media Import window, as the name implies, is the place where you bring media into Final Cut Pro X, either from Camera or Devices or external hard drive. Be aware when referring to camera, this also means the media cards used inside of cameras.

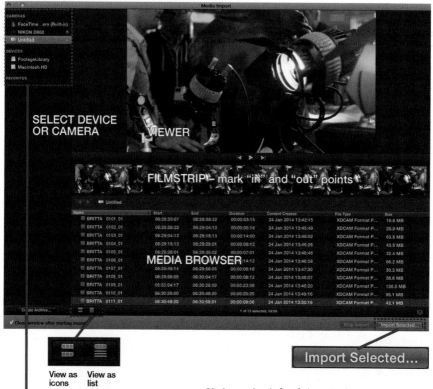

Import Selected...

View as icons View as list

Click on the left of the Media Import Window and select a Camera or Device.

In the case of the example to the left there are three camera options:

(i) FaceTime—record live off the built-in camera in the MacBook Pro.

(ii) Nikon D800—media card from DSLR.

(iii) Untitled—this is a Sony SxS card denoted by the SxS icon.

Importing from Camera or Media Card

As written, the Media Import window is the place where you bring media into Final Cut Pro X from camera, device, media card or hard drive. When accessing media from camera or media cards, in most cases, it is as simple as connecting the camera or media card, inside of a card reader, to the computer. You then open up the Media Import window, select the clips you wish to import—and then press the Import Selected button. Below is a run-through of the process.

1   Connect Camera or Media Card to your Mac.

2   Open the Media Import Window (shortcut Command + i).

3   Highlight the Camera or Card.

4   Click on a clip in the Media Browser and this will then show in the Viewer.

5   You can view the clips by skimming through the media. Press the letter S if skimming is not switched on.

You can selectively choose clips, and import these individually, or choose multiple clips, or choose to Import All of the media.

The simplest way to get the media onto the hard drive is to press the Import All command (at the bottom right of the Camera Import window). All of the clips will then be written to the hard drive where the Events folder is located. Note: you need to have Copy Media to Event Folder checked in Import Preferences.

You can also be selective about which clips are transferred. For a single clip, click to highlight the clip of choice and press Import Selected.

You can highlight a section of a single clip to import by either dragging the yellow ends to mark the range of media you wish to import or pressing the letter "i" for in and "o" for out to define the beginning and end points.

To import multiple clips, press the Command key (immediately left of the space bar) and click to highlight those clips you wish to import. Once the clips are highlighted, press Import Selected.

Regardless of whether you choose to import a single clip, a section of a clip, multiple clips, or all of the clips, you need to define some crucial details before the media is written to drive.

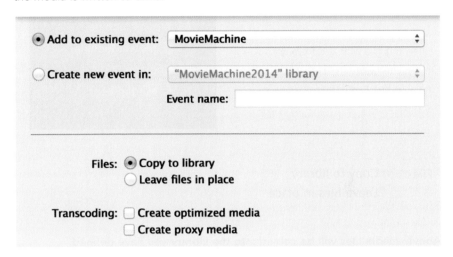

You now have a choice—you can either add the clips you are importing to an existing Event; or you can choose to create a New Event.

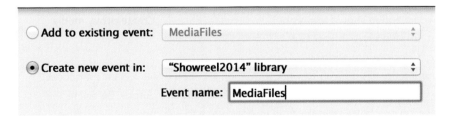

Always remember, media is filed away inside of Events which live inside of a Library. Therefore, it is advisable to have created a named Library with an Event before you begin the Import Process.

If you do choose to create a new Event you need to choose the Library in which the Event will be stored. You also need to name the Event.

Effectively you are telling Final Cut Pro X where you wish the media to be filed away, so you can then access this within the Browser.

The other hugely important instruction you need to give to Final Cut Pro X is to define where the media files are to be stored. The media files can be stored within the Library itself, as described earlier, this is a Managed Library. Or you can Leave in Place which means Final Cut Pro X will then reference to the media.

Above: media files will be copied into the Library you have defined.

These options, provided on import, are very similar to those options given in the Import area of Preferences. You will encounter these choices time and time again working in Final Cut Pro X, so it is worth getting to know the choices and how to deal with them!

There are other important choices to consider—again these mirror options already presented when you set up the Import Preferences.

You need to choose if you wish to create Optimized Media. Some say this option should always be left on—therefore if Final Cut Pro X decides the codec is computationally difficult to work with, then the media files will be transcoded to ProRes which is ideal for Final Cut Pro X to edit and output. Be aware that transcoding of files will take time to generate and will consume hard drive space.

Often I will choose to leave the Create optimized media option off—you can always choose to transcode at a later stage if you wish, and, the truth is, Final Cut Pro X does an admirable job of editing and playing back most modern codecs. Therefore the option is always there to transcode at any stage, whether you selected for this to be done on import or not.

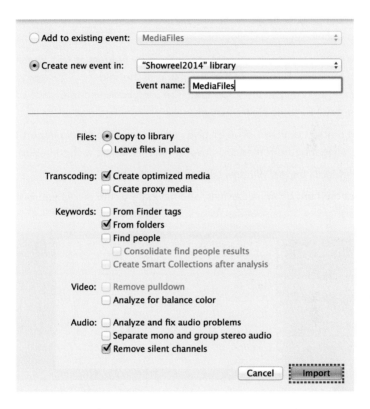

The rest of the options I leave switched off. Most of the time I'm not using Proxy media—and if I choose to use Proxy media I can generate these files when I need them, rather than on Import. I leave the other options off as I don't wish for the editing software to Analyze for color balance, to Find people, or to work on my audio. These are all things I can do myself.

Once you have defined the choices press Import and the files will be written to hard drive, into the Event you specified, within the Library you have chosen.

Importing Media from Hard Drive

The process of importing media which already exists on hard drive is very similar to bringing in from Camera or Media card, however, there are a few key differences.

First, you cannot bring in a portion of a clip, the entire clip is imported. Beyond this, when bringing in media which already exists inside of a folder you can choose to define Keyword Collections by name of the Folder.

This same option—where Keywords are defined by Folders, is also found in the Import Preferences. This means that the name of the folder will be assigned to the collection of clips you are importing. The usefulness and relevance of Keywording will become clear in Chapter 4.

To import media from hard drive involves opening up the Media Import Window and then navigating from the hard drive to the media you wish to import.

1   Open Media Import Window (shortcut Command + i).

2   Select the hard drive, in Devices, and navigate to the media you wish to import.

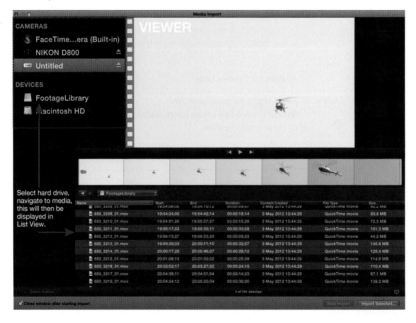

3   Highlight the clips you wish to Import or you can Import All. Clips are displayed in List View. When importing from hard drive Icon View is unavailable.

The familiar window will now appear where you need to define important details.

● Add to existing event:	MediaFiles ⬍
○ Create new event in:	"MovieMachine2014" library ⬍
	Event name:

Files: ○ Copy to library
● Leave files in place

Transcoding: ☐ Create optimized media
☐ Create proxy media

Keywords: ☐ From Finder tags
☑ From folders
☐ Find people
☐ Consolidate find people results
☐ Create Smart Collections after analysis

Video: ☐ Remove pulldown
☐ Analyze for balance color

Audio: ☐ Analyze and fix audio problems
☐ Separate mono and group stereo audio
☑ Remove silent channels

Cancel   Import

You will recognize these choices from importing from Card or Camera.

Most important, choose if you are to Add the media to an existing Event—or if you wish to create a new Event, and if so, where this will be located.

Equally important, decide if you want the files to be copied to the Library or choose Leave in Place.

To reinforce what has already been written, choose to Leave in Place—this means no media is copied and the files are then referenced to in the location where they currently exist. If you choose this option it is vital that you know where the media is located and make sure that it doesn't get moved or deleted! If this happens you can lose the files forever.

I leave Keywords: From Folders selected. This is very useful for organizing media. It is advisable to therefore name folders which you

are importing with an appropriate name as this information will then be included as the name of the Keyword Collection. Much more on Keywording coming up!

The other choices I leave unchecked.

4   Press Import and the files will be brought into Final Cut Pro X and, if required, will then be copied and written to drive.

When you import media, you will get a display showing the files are being processed.

The Dashboard shows when the computer is working.

Look to the Dashboard and bang in the center of the interface—if you see a spinning wheel, you will know media is being processed. It may be that rendering is taking place, the computer may be generating thumbnails, or media may be transcoding. The Dashboard indicator will display a spinning circle or show a percentage symbol to show that work is being done in the background.

Click on the spinning wheel in the Dashboard to reveal which processes are taking place.

Capture from Tape

There is a third way to bring in media: Final Cut Pro X enables capture from DV, DVCAM, or HDV tape.

For those who shoot these formats, or those who have an archive to be accessed, this facility enables the media to be transferred to a hard drive. The transfer facility is basic but effective.

1 Plug your camera into the Mac with a FireWire cable or with a Thunderbolt to FireWire adapter.

2 Set the camera to VTR mode, then turn it on. Check that the camera is outputting the format you wish to capture, that is, DV/DVCAM or HDV. If the camera is not set correctly, Final Cut Pro X will not see the video signal.

3 Turn your attention to Final Cut Pro X and press the camera icon or choose Import from Camera from the File menu.

4 The Media Import window will open.

Note: You can see that the FireWire device is recognized as it will appear in the list of cameras. You can also capture live from the built-in camera when using a laptop and record direct to hard drive.

5 Play the tape using the virtual VTR controller. Alternatively, use the Space Bar for start/stop, the letter J to spool backward (press J up to five times to spool) and the letter L to spool forwards (again incrementally up to five taps of the L key).

Press Import and you will see the familiar window prompting you to define several fields of information.

As with previous importing you need to define if the media is to be added to an Existing Event or if you wish to create a new Event; do you wish to copy files into the selected Library or another location; and other details such as whether you wish to create Proxy Media. By now these should be familiar choices.

Importing to Events by dragging

There is a fourth and final way to import media into Final Cut Pro X. This only works for media which already exists on hard drive.

You can literally drag and drop files from a location on hard drive, be it an entire folder or individual clips, direct onto an Event. The files will then be added to the Event—with the options for how the media is handled, in terms of Media Storage, Transcoding and other options being defined by the choices you made when you set the Import Preferences.

This is possibly the most simple way of bringing media into Final Cut Pro X and the method I use regularly. Simply locate media files on hard drive, drag these onto an Event to the left of the Browser, and these will then be included with media within the Event. Drag entire folders of media to an Event and the same applies and, if you have selected Keywords: From

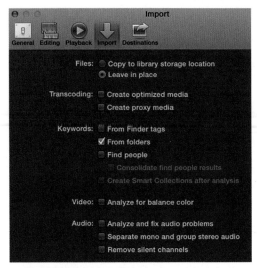

Folders in Import Preferences, the name of the folder will then determine the naming of the Keyword Collection.

Drag files direct from hard drive to an Event and the media will then be added to the Event. You can drag individual or multiple files, or an entire Folder which contains the media.

 Library

In the above example an entire folder is dragged into an Event—Events live inside of a Library and within an Event is where the detailed work of cataloguing the media takes place.

 Event

●RGANIZATION

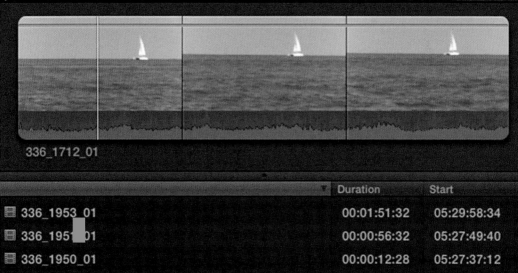

ips ‡

336_1712_01

	▼	Duration	Start	
336_1953_01		00:01:51:32	05:29:58:34	
336_1951_01		00:00:56:32	05:27:49:40	
336_1950_01		00:00:12:28	05:27:37:12	
336_1949_01		00:00:11:56	05:27:25:16	
336_1948_01		00:00:26:50	05:26:58:26	
336_1715_01		00:00:49:00	03:59:45:20	
336_1714_01		00:00:26:00	03:59:19:20	
336_1713_01		00:00:12:32	03:59:07:04	
336_1712_01		00:00:22:50	03:58:44:14	

Organizational concepts within Final Cut Pro X

The critical thing to understand when it comes to organization within Final Cut Pro X is that the structure of **Library—Events—Keywords** and **Projects** is the foundation of all organization within Final Cut Pro X.

The Library is the master area at the top of the organizational level. This is saved to hard drive, so that you can locate it when you need it.

My method is to save the Library to the same hard drive where the media exists. Most of the time my media already exists on hard drive and therefore when media is imported I choose Leave files in place. By saving the Library to the same external drive as the media, I ensure that both Library and Media exist in the same place.

| | Library | | | Event | | | Keyword Collection |

Anytime I need to open a Library in Final Cut Pro X, I simply connect up the drive, which contains the Library and the Media, and double click the Library to open it. The result is the Library, with Events, Projects and Media, opens in Final Cut Pro X.

I will often have many different Libraries on a given hard drive and many media folders.

Libraries located on hard drive.

Media Folders on hard drive.

Here you can see the relationship between the Libraries in the Final Cut Pro X interface, and the same Libraries as they exist on hard drive. The easiest way to open a particular Library is to locate it on hard drive and double click it.

FINAL CUT PRO X
INTERFACE

Footage Compile ——— Library

Places

Antarctica
MauiHawaii
Rome ——— Event
Scarborough
Scotland

Morooco Event Filming

Morocco Footage ——— Keyword Collection

Within each of the Libraries are Events and Keyword Collections. The Events are collections of media which you have imported, whereas Keyword Collections are those same collections organized into more accessible, defined areas—a similar concept to working with Bins in other NLE applications.

My method of working is to create a Library for a particular job or edit—for example, I may be editing a training video for one client—that becomes a Library; for another client I'm editing a documentary—that is another Library; for another client a promotional video—that becomes another Library.

Projects are stored inside of the Events; the Events are stored within a Library. Projects can be accessed within the Library or the Event in which they were created. The Projects are the edited timelines of media which make up your edits.

Projects, along with media, can be viewed in List View or Icon View by pressing the controls at the bottom of the Event Library.

 List View

 Icon View

Essentially, the file system provided within Final Cut Pro X, for **Library—Events—Keyword Collections** and **Projects**, gives you a sophisticated way to work with large quantities of media in an ordered way.

For now I'm outlining concepts. There is no correct or incorrect way to manage how you work—so long as you are organized and can access the media to edit your movies. Final Cut Pro X provides the means for you to be exceptionally organized and gives you tools to edit to the highest levels. It is for you to build your own systems and make the software work for you.

Creating Libraries, Events and Projects

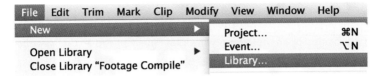

You can only create a Library from the File menu top-left of the Final Cut Pro X interface. Choose New—Library.

There is no shortcut to do this and no other way than by going to the File menu.

I suspect the reason there is only one way to achieve this, with no shortcut, is because Apple wants the editor to consider carefully when creating a Library. You don't want Libraries scattered all over the place—these are master places which include the entire foundation and structure of your project, media, or references to media, and everything connected with it. Therefore, when creating a Library consider how the Library will used. Better to be organized at the beginning rather than having to sort out a mess later on.

Creating Events and Projects can also be done from the File menu, or control-click in the Events Browser and choose the appropriate option. You can also use shortcuts:

Command + N	New Project.
Alt/Option + N	New Event.

New Event ⌥N
New Project ⌘N
New Folder ⇧⌘N
New Keyword Collection ⇧⌘K

Control-click in an Event to show menu choices.

You can also close a Library or several Libraries. The rule is at least one Library must be open at any given time. It can make perfect sense to work with only a single Library open, for the very reason that all Projects and related media will then be before you, without the confusion of other Libraries. You do not need to work with multiple Libraries open unless you choose to.

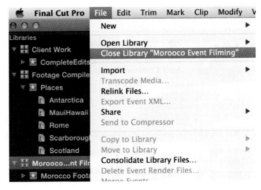

Control-click a Library and choose Close Library or choose this command from the File menu

However, you do need to know how to find and track down Libraries which you do not have open.

By default Final Cut Pro X returns to the state you left it when you last quit. So if you had 5 Libraries open, next time you open Final Cut Pro X, the same 5 Libraries will open—assuming the drives and media are connected to your Mac.

To open and access available Libraries choose File—Open Library—and the most recent Libraries opened will be listed before you.

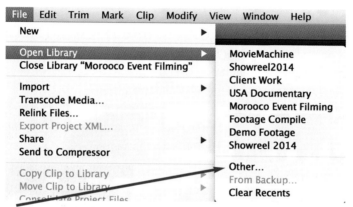

Press Other and the Open Library window will appear, giving you access to available Libraries. At this point you can choose a Library from the list in front of you, or choose New to create a New Library, or press Locate to manually navigate to a Library you wish to open.

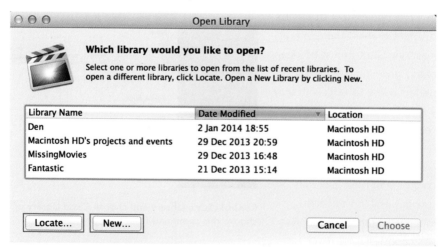

To close a Library click the Library to highlight then either: (i) Choose File—Close Library (ii) Control-click the Library and select the command Close Library.

Perhaps the easiest way to open a Library, already mentioned and the way I work, is to locate the Library at the Finder level—this means on hard drive, or wherever it is located, and simply double-click the Library Bundle. The Library will then open in Final Cut Pro X and you can access all the Events with media and Projects within the Library.

You can easily delete an Event—simply Control-click on the Event and choose Move Event to Trash.

To remove a Project Control-click the Project and choose Move to Trash.

To remove a Keyword Collection Control-click the Keyword Collection and choose Delete Keyword Collection.

The only way to delete a Library is to locate the Library on hard drive, drag it to the Trash, and then empty the Trash. It is best to quit Final Cut Pro X before doing this.

If the concepts of Libraries, Events, Projects and Keyword Collections are abstract and confusing, the meaning of these will soon become clear as we begin the process of organizing media using Events and Keyword Collections.

Getting practical: hands-on reviewing and organizing of footage

To make the editing process efficient and streamlined, you need to be organized. Organization is the key to building, refining, and sculpting a film. You need to know where those clips are, how to access them, and how to get them into the Timeline to hit the mark every time. There are many tools within Final Cut Pro X to help you to organize your footage. The process of getting organized begins with reviewing your footage.

You can change the display of clips within the Browser. Click the icon bottom right which will display the control to switch on or off Audio Waveforms. This only works in icon view.

Press to reveal Clip Appearance

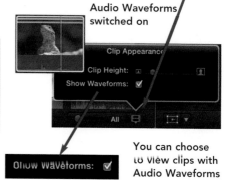

You can choose to view clips with Audio Waveforms

Reviewing Footage

1 Select an Event in the Event Library and click any of the clips in the Event. The clip you select will then show in the Viewer.

2 Press the Space Bar and the clip will play. Press the Space Bar again to stop.

3 You can also use the letters J, K, and L to review footage. By tapping J or L, the footage will play, then speed up, incrementally, each time you press the key (up to five taps).

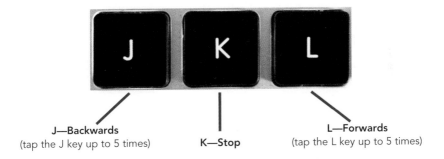

J—Backwards
(tap the J key up to 5 times)

K—Stop

L—Forwards
(tap the L key up to 5 times)

4 Perhaps the easiest way to look through a clip is to use the Skimming function. Simply point the curser towards any of the clips in the Event Library

SKIMMER BAR

and drag across it. You will see the clip zip past in fast motion in the Viewer as you drag. If this doesn't work, press the letter S to activate Skimming.

EVENT LIBRARY

Drag across clips in the Event Library and see the result in the Viewer.

Expand the filmstrip size using the controls bottom right of the Event Library. This gives you fine control while skimming over a clip.

- S: Skimming (toggles on/off).
- Shift + S: Skimming without audio (toggle on/off).

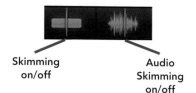

Skimming on/off   Audio Skimming on/off

Use the above shortcuts or use the Skimming controls in the middle/right of the interface.

Note: When using the Skimming feature you can drag across several clips; you don't need to do this one at a time.

With several clips lined up in the Event Library, skim across as many as you wish to view—you will then see the footage displayed in the Viewer as you skim.

Rating Footage

The ability to rate your footage provides a fantastic means to weed out the good footage from the bad. Clips can be marked as Favorites, Rejects, or left unrated.

You don't have to rate your footage. If you have a photographic memory and can remember everything by the sheer power of thought, then fantastic for you; however, most of us need to constantly review the media to remind us where everything is. Being able to mark specific clips as good or bad can be very useful.

Below the Event Library, notice two stars and a red cross. These are your rating tools.

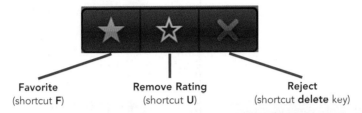

Favorite	Remove Rating	Reject
(shortcut **F**)	(shortcut **U**)	(shortcut **delete** key)

Highlight a clip in the Event Viewer and skim through it. Decide whether the clip is one you want to use or is one you want to reject.

If it is a clip you wish to mark as a Favorite, press the green star below the Event Library or press the letter F. If you are in Filmstrip view, a green line will appear within the clip. If you are in List view—click the triangle to the left of the clip you marked and Favorite will be marked below the clip.

Green line indicates Favorite.

Red line indicates Reject.

Should you wish to mark a clip as a Reject press the red X or the Delete key. In Filmstrip view, the clip is marked red; in List view, this is indicated below the clip as a red X.

Note: The blue line you can see marked in each of the clips represents that a Keyword has been added to that clip. More on Keywording coming up!

There is a good reason to go to the effort of marking clips as Favorites or Rejects.

Click the drop-down menu in the top left corner of the Event Viewer interface and you see options to sort media within the Event.

You can choose to Hide Rejected clips, immediately eliminating anything from view which you have marked as Rejected.

You can also choose to show only Favorites—those clips you have marked as being good takes.

Alternatively, you can choose to only show the Rejected media—perhaps you are deep into editing and need just one more shot . . . so you start looking through the media which you initially rejected.

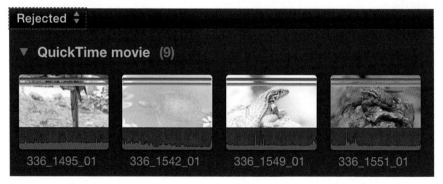

I'm sure the advantages are clear of being able to rate and show only the Favorites or hide the Rejected clips. Effectively what Apple has created is a functional database geared to define footage as good or bad.

Remember to reset to All Clips, as the setting you choose will remain until you change it, even when you move between different Events.

You can choose to use or reject this functionality. I find it useful and it gets much deeper than simply marking clips as Favorites or Rejects.

Marking Sections within Clips

Not only can you mark Favorites and Rejects, you can also selectively mark sections within clips as Favorites or Rejects, and then use the sort options to show only the portions of the clip you specify.

This is particularly useful when dealing with long clips. For example, a 20-minute interview can be marked up at the most relevant places, or a three-hour conference record could be marked for the highlights of the piece only.

Here's how it works:

1 Skim through a clip in the Events Browser.

2 Click on the clip then drag the yellow range markers to define the area you wish to select. Alternatively, use the letter "i" for in and "o" for out to define the area.

Drag the yellow range markers to define the range within the clip or press the letters I O F in succession to mark a range selection.

3 Press F to mark this section as a Favorite or press the Delete key to mark as Rejected. Alternatively, use the green star for Favorite and red cross for Reject.

Favorite

Reject

As you mark the sections, observe that only the portions you defined are marked as a Favorite or Reject.

Multiple favourites marked within a single clip

A mixture of Favorites and Rejects can be marked within a single clip.

Note the different views: List view (above) and filmstrip (left). Favorites and rejects are clearly marked.

You can then selectively display Favorites or Rejects from the filtering choices at the top right of the Event Viewer.

It should be clear that the ability to mark clips and sections within clips as Favorites or Rejects, and then be able to sort this information, is of tremendous benefit, particularly when you are dealing with a lot of media, or when many long takes have been recorded. You can mark entire takes as good or bad or sections within takes.

This ability to mark and sort is one of the great strengths of Final Cut Pro X.

Labeling and Searching Clips

In all the images shown so far, each of the clips have had names assigned by the camera during filming.

None of these numbers mean very much, other than being a sequential naming of the clips.

Final Cut Pro X offers a powerful means to name and then search through all of the named clips. You can also easily add comments which can be searched, and, if you wish, you can Batch Rename clips. In terms of being organized, this is of huge importance. You can quickly search through all of the Events on your computer to locate any of the named clips.

Labeling clips is easy. You can work in either Filmstrip or List view.

1   Click on a clip to highlight, then click on the naming area so you can overtype.

2   Type a name relevant to the clip.

3   Press return.

4   Repeat the process for other clips in the Event which you wish to rename.

In the following images, there are several different views of a lizard. Each has been individually named by following the above steps. The real magic is in the search abilities of Final Cut Pro X. Each of the clips that has been named is searchable; therefore, if we key in the word "lizard" into the search criteria in the top right of the Browser, then any matching items will be found.

Each of the clips has been named so that it can be searched through using the database capabilities of Final Cut Pro X.

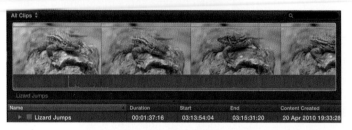

Key in the search criteria (top right of the Events Browser) and matching items will be displayed in either List or Filmstrip view.

Above: the search criteria displayed in Filmstrip view.

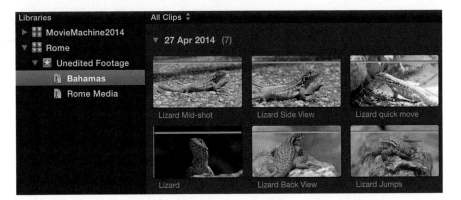

It is important to be aware that every time you search, the results will be displayed according to whether you click a Library or an Event or a Keyword Collection.

You therefore selectively display the media you choose to look at. Editing is about honing in on what you need, and avoiding that which is not needed.

By effectively naming clips enables us to then use the Search ability within Final Cut Pro X to pin-point exactly what is needed.

Adding Notes to Clips

Notes can be just as useful as adding name labels to your clips. Quite often, when scanning through footage, I will stop and add a quick comment to a clip. It may be as simple as "great shot" or "definitely use," or something more specific like "nice, light—evening," or perhaps "use in end sequence."

Anything that will stick in my memory which I can then key into the search field to retrieve the shot when I need it.

Go into List view in the Events Browser; observe that there are several columns extending to the right. Control-click and add the column titled Notes.

Control click to add the column titled Notes.

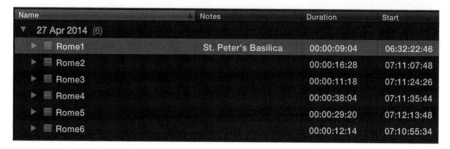

Click and drag so the Notes column sits next to the Name column.

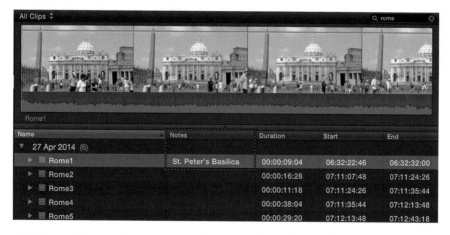

Click in the Notes column (to the right of any of the clips) and type information. You can enter anything from a single word to detailed descriptions.

Everything you type becomes searchable. Once you have entered information for several clips, then type a word you wish to search for into the Search Criteria area, at the top right of the Events Browser.

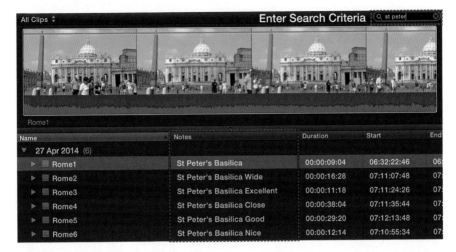

All of the information entered as notes is searchable.

The clips with matching results will then be displayed for you to work with.

Note how the order of search takes place. If you click on a Library then the Library will be searched; click on an Event and the Event will be searched; likewise, click on a Keyword Collection and the Keyword Collection will be searched.

You have powerful database capabilities at your fingertips to search through notes and clip names, provided you go to the effort of organizing and marking up your footage.

Batch Renaming of Clips

The ability to Batch Rename clips in Final Cut Pro X is a fantastic means for the editor to organize their footage, not just because naming conventions like 013_0251_01 for camera originals is meaningless and useless, but also because clips which you have renamed are searchable.

Batch renaming enables you to set the naming convention and then instruct Final Cut Pro to rename the clips you have chosen. Once done, you can search through all of the Events stored within a Library to access all of the clips which you have renamed. This is a fantastic way to give meaningful names to your media for quick access, and to see at a glance, in either List or Filmstrip view, what the names of each of the clips refer to.

1. To Batch Rename clips, you need to first set the naming convention. Press the icon to open the Inspector or shortcut Command + 4.

2. To the bottom of the Info tab of the Inspector, click Apply Custom Name then scroll to Edit.

3 You will be greeted with a very complicated window, shown below. Click to choose the second option on the left, which is Custom Name with Counter.

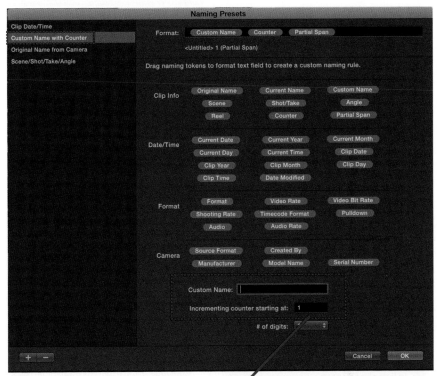

4 Click in the Custom Name box and type the naming convention you wish to use. Notice the increments you define will start at the number 1 unless you choose otherwise.

5 Now highlight a number of clips in any of your Events.

6 Go to the Info tab of the Inspector and at the bottom select Apply Custom Name—then choose Custom Name with Counter.

The clips which you highlighted have then been renamed in the Event.

7 Repeat the process to change the naming preset and then you can Batch Rename other groups of clips. You can now search through all of the clips on any of the drives connected to your Mac.

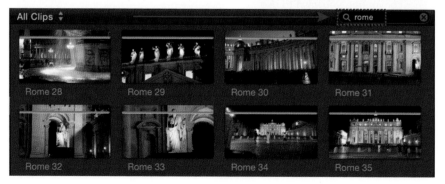

8 Click to highlight a Library, Event or Keyword Collection. Type the search criteria into the top right of the Browser. You can then view the clips that match your search term.

▶ ▤ Rome 28	00:00:16:06	19:27:40:00	19:27:56:06
▶ ▤ Rome 29	00:00:30:13	19:33:34:00	19:34:04:13
▶ ▤ Rome 30	00:00:33:02	19:28:59:00	19:29:32:02
▶ ▤ Rome 31	00:00:21:11	19:37:10:00	19:37:31:11
▶ ▤ Rome 32	00:00:02:21	19:38:11:00	19:38:13:21
▶ ▤ Rome 33	00:00:10:22	19:40:01:00	19:40:11:22
▶ ▤ Rome 34	00:00:15:06	19:44:51:00	19:45:06:06
▶ ▤ Rome 35	00:00:17:06	19:45:26:00	19:45:43:06
▶ ▤ Rome 36	00:00:12:16	19:47:32:00	19:47:44:16
▶ ▤ Rome 37	00:02:07:02	20:03:46:00	20:05:53:02

Clips that match the search criteria can then be viewed in either Filmstrip or List view. You therefore have a very simple means to Batch Rename clips and search through all of your Events to find exactly what you want, according to the naming structure you have chosen.

Keywording

If you want to get really sophisticated with the organization of your media, step into the world of Keywording. I think of rating footage, or marking Favorites and Rejects, as being a simple way to organize your footage. Keywording gives you far greater power.

Do not feel under pressure to keyword. Many editors are happy to break footage into labeled events, perhaps rate or define sections as Favorites, and leave it at that. The power of Keywording is that within a single Event you can break your footage into defined sections, known as Keyword Collections. Think of Keyword Collections as a means to file footage away, or to break it into manageable, accessible groups.

Keywording can be applied to an entire clip, a range within a clip, or a group of clips.

Adding Keywords is done through what is known as the Keyword Editor.

1   Press Command + K to open the Keyword Editor or press the Key symbol to the middle left of the Final Cut Pro X interface.

Press Command + K or
press the Key symbol to the
left of the Toolbar to open
the Keyword Editor

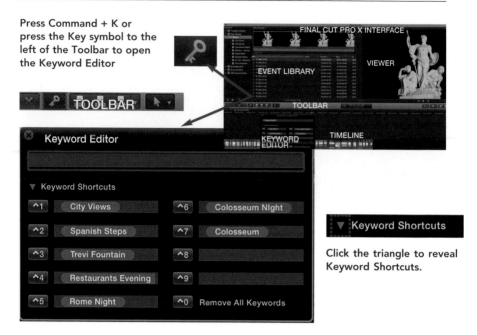

The Keyword Editor will open in front of you. This may or may not have
Keywords entered into it depending on whether or not you have used this
before.

2   Highlight a clip or a group of clips which you wish to apply the Keyword to.

3   Type the Keyword into the Keyword Editor,
    then press Return. The Keyword will then be
    applied to the media you selected.

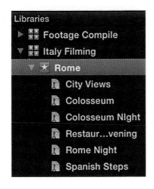

In the case to the left there are many Keyword collections all contained within a single Event.

Essentially all of the media contained in the Event—Rome—has been broken down into smaller collections to make locating specific media easier to achieve.

A blue line through each of the clips indicates that a Keyword has been applied.

Keywords can also be added using shortcuts. First, open the Keyword Editor, then press the triangle to reveal the list of Keywords; the short-cut is located to the left of each of the Keywords. As you type a few letters relevant Keywords will appear.

Shortcut to enter Keywords
Control + 1 through to 9

Shortcut to clear all Keywords
Control + 0

Type to enter Keywords or use the shortcuts. Highlight a clip or clips in the Browser and press shortcut Control + 1 through to 9 to quickly add the Keywords already entered into the Keyword editor.

To clear Keywords from media with Keywords already applied, highlight a clip or group of clips and press Control + 0 this deletes all Keywords. This works whether the Keyword Editor is open or not.

To remove Keywords from the shortcut area of the Keyword Editor click on the Keyword within the editor and press delete.

When many Keyword Collections have been added, you end up with many categories, defined by yourself, where media is filed away. Be aware, Keyword Collections apply to a single Event, therefore, it can make sense to put all related media, or even all the media for a project into a single Event, and then break it up into Keyword Collections.

Keywording can be applied to groups of clips, individual clips, or a range within a clip.

You can selectively apply a Keyword to part of a clip by marking a Range before applying the Keyword.

To apply a Keyword to a range in a clip, highlight the Clip, use the yellow range selectors to define the area in the clip, then apply the Keyword.

As stated earlier, you do not have to Keyword your media. However, once you understand the concept of Keywording you will find, particularly on a project with lots of media, that this can be a great timesaver. Once upon a time, the only way to log your footage was to write notes, watch footage in real time, and jot down timecode numbers. Keywording provides a sophisticated means to log your footage, file it away, and retrieve it when you need to get to it quickly.

In summary, notice an entire chapter, more than 20 pages, has been devoted to organization. This is because it is essential for the editor to be organized. You can't edit a production effectively without being organized.

Many years ago, in tape suites, the method was a paper edit with burnt-in timecode as a reference. The producer would come into the edit suite with pages of notes after having worked through the raw material in an offline suite or even viewing on VHS tape. Edit suites were expensive, so the time needed in these rooms was minimized.

Now, we have a world of tools to prepare, organize, and edit our media. The temptation may be to skip the organizing and sorting of footage, avoid Keywords, adding notes or clip names. My view is that it is counterproductive for you not to be organized. I use a combination of all the methods described: Keywording, Batch Renaming, and adding notes to clips. This proves to be incredibly useful throughout the editing process. I regard the organization phase as laying the foundation for the edit. Spend the time getting organized and the rest of the edit will fall together.

EDITING

Editing is, without doubt, one of the most wonderfully creative art forms of the twentieth century, and has evolved into a universal means of expression in the twenty-first century. Previously, editing was restricted to those who worked in TV stations, those who worked in the film industry, and independent filmmakers, groups, and companies. Now, it's a totally different scene. Twenty-first century editing gives the tools to anyone to create amazingly high-quality video.

Jump back 30 or 40 years. Unless you were a professional, or rich, you were most likely going to be working with Super 8. Super 8 was affordable, accessible, and referred to as spaghetti by those in the industry. The size of the frame was one-quarter that of 16 mm, which, itself, was one-quarter that of 35 mm. So working with Super 8 was not only fiddly and awkward, the quality suffered.

Working with Final Cut Pro X the quality does not suffer! This is a capable editing system which outputs many high-end codecs, including ProRes at either standard, HQ, LT, or even ProRes 4:4:4. ProRes is a high-quality mastering format with several levels of quality:

ProRes LT:	100 Mbps
ProRes standard:	145 Mbps
ProRes HQ:	220 Mbps
ProRes 4:4:4:	Cinema quality
ProRes XQ:	500 Mbps used for mastering and high-end cinema work

ProRes 4:4:4 is cinema quality—get that? This is a big deal. Back in the days of editing Super 8 or 16 mm anyone would have jumped at this opportunity.

The fact that Final Cut Pro X can produce cinema quality is a big deal! Back in the days of editing Super 8 or 16 mm many would have jumped at this opportunity!

Regardless of the level at which you work, the mechanics behind post-producing your movie are the same.

The Process

Before we begin editing, let us quickly run through the process. Whether you're editing a home movie or a feature film, the process is the same.

i   Get footage onto hard drive.

ii   Review and look at the footage, get to know it, file it, and categorize it so you can extract what you need.

iii   Do a picture edit, meaning cut it all together. Often, a soundtrack and picture edit are built at the same time.

iv   Attend to audio—do what you can to make it sound good.

v   Add effects. This may also be done during the editing process. Effects can be as simple as a basic title to complex, multilayered effects which have been carefully built and constructed. Final Cut Pro X offers a wide range of pre-built and customizable effects.

vi   Output—you may need to output a high-resolution QuickTime file, an H.264 encode, DVD, or Blu-ray. The means to output at a professional level is fully provided.

So far, we have covered importing footage to hard drive, reviewing, and organizing the footage.

Now, the time has come to start the editing process.

Creating a New Project

This is a very simple and essential procedure. You need to create a project—your movie, your edit, your Timeline—whatever you want to call it, the Project contains all the information which makes up the edited content.

1   Control-click on a Library or an Event and choose New Project, or, highlight the Event and choose File—New Project. You will then be prompted to name the Project and confirm the Event where the Project will exist.

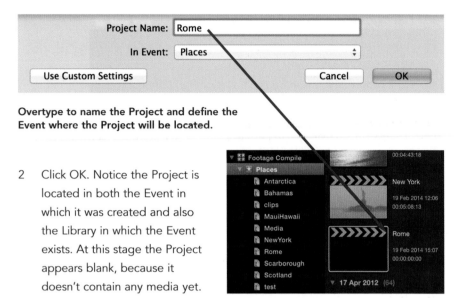

| Project Name: | Rome |
| In Event: | Places |

Use Custom Settings   Cancel   OK

Overtype to name the Project and define the Event where the Project will be located.

2   Click OK. Notice the Project is located in both the Event in which it was created and also the Library in which the Event exists. At this stage the Project appears blank, because it doesn't contain any media yet.

This is the easy way to create a project—the project attributes will be determined by the first clip which is then edited into project Timeline.

Easy is not always best! If you choose Use Custom Settings a window will open and you then have **Use Custom Settings** more control over project attributes such as Format, Resolution and Frame-rate.

Project Name:	Rome
In Event:	Places
Starting Timecode:	00:00:00;00
Video Properties:	● Set based on first video clip
	○ Custom
Audio and Render Properties:	● Use default settings
	Stereo, 48kHz, ProRes 422
	○ Custom

Use Automatic Settings   Cancel   OK

You need to know what format and frame rate you wish to output. In the world of HD, there are two main standards: 1280 x 720 or 1920 x 1080 (often called 720P and 1080P), and each of these can run at different frame rates.

By letting Final Cut Pro X automatically set the video properties based on the first clip, this means, if you edit a 1920 x 1080 clip as the first clip into the Timeline, the result will be you will be editing a 1920 x 1080 project (at the frame rate of the first clip dropped into the Timeline).

If the first clip is 1280 x 720, then you will effectively be setting the project to be a 1280 x 720 project. It may be that you are working with 4:3 DV footage—again, if the first clip is set to this standard, then that is the image size which will be set.

Video Properties: ⦿ Set based on first video clip

Very often projects are made up of a mixture of footage—some HD, some SD, and perhaps a mixture of widescreen and standard aspect ratio. Furthermore, some footage may be shot at 25 frames per second, other footage at 29.97, and perhaps some at 24P. If you let the computer set the video properties automatically, then you need to make sure the first clip you edit into the Timeline is of the frame size and frame rate you wish to output to.

The idea of letting the computer set the video properties automatically is designed to make life easy, not complex. If all or the majority of the footage you are working with is of one standard, then allowing this to be set automatically can be a good idea.

There are times when it is advantageous to set the video properties manually. This gives you power to define the format, frame size, and frame rate.

Manually Setting Up a Project

I often choose to work this way. By manually setting up the project you can define details such as format, resolution, and frame rate.

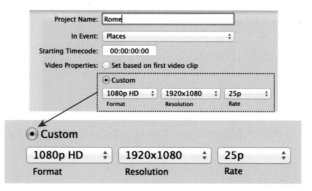

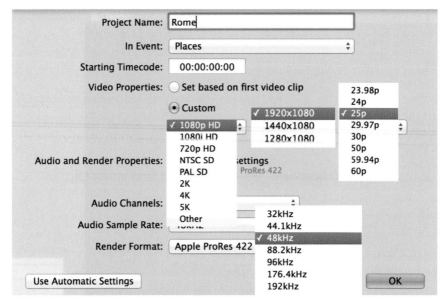

You can also choose to manually set up the audio and you can define the render format.

If these settings, numbers, frame rates, and different standards are completely confusing to you, then you need to stick to automatic. For those who have a good technical understanding of video production, setting up a project manually can often be the best way forward.

Once the project settings have been chosen, make sure the project is named, and press OK. You are now ready to move onto your first edit.

Basic Cutting

As already described, there are three areas you need to work among: the Events Library, the Viewer, and the Timeline.

You access clips in the Events Library, you watch these in the Viewer, and then you edit into the Timeline; and it is there the building blocks which represent the clips of your edit are organized.

1 Choose a clip inside one of the events.

2 Click on the clip and skim through it (press S if Skimming does not work).

3 Define a range within the clip by dragging either of the yellow ends or by pressing I and O.

Press "i" to mark in.
Press "o" to mark out.

EMPTY TIMELINE

4 Once a range is defined, look to the empty Timeline. Press the letter E. You will see the shot you highlighted in the Events Browser has been edited into the Timeline. How this is represented in the Timeline is determined by the view you have set for the Clip Appearance.

Click bottom right of the Timeline to reveal options for Clip Appearance.

A SINGLE SHOT HAS BEEN
EDITED INTO THE TIMELINE

5 Repeat the procedure—select a shot, view by skimming, mark a range, press the letter E (for Edit or for End) and the next shot will be edited to the end of the Timeline. This type of edit is referred to as an Append edit.

2 SHOTS EDITED INTO THE TIMELINE

6 Repeat the procedure until you will have several shots cut together in the Timeline.

SEVERAL SHOTS IN THE TIMELINE

Note: If you highlight several clips in the Browser and press E, then these are edited in order direct into the Timeline.

MVI_6163   MVI_6166   MVI_6180   MVI_6156

Highlight clips and edit these direct into the Timeline.

Notice that each clip is made up of video and audio. Video and audio are locked together, indicating the synchronization of image and sound.

Switch on Show Waveforms in Clip Appearance.

Clips in the Timeline can be displayed in several different ways according to your choice for clip appearance.

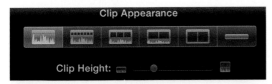

Click the icon bottom right of the Timeline to reveal options for Clip Appearance.

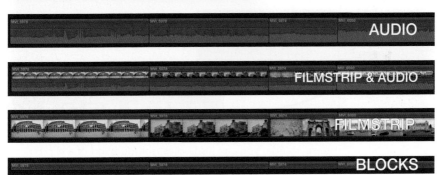

Sliding Clips around in the Timeline

You will now have several clips in the Timeline. These are in the order which you edited them. This ordering can quickly and easily be rearranged.

You can use the slider bottom right on the Timeline window to adjust the spread of the clips in the Timeline. This only affects the appearance, not duration.

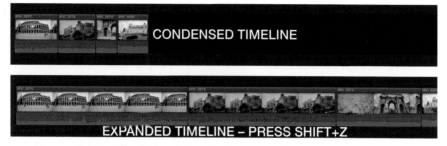

Press Shift + Z to fit the entire contents of the Timeline into the available space. Doing this makes it easy to get an overview of everything that has been edited into the Timeline.

To rearrange the shots simply click on a clip, drag it to a new position within the Timeline between two other clips, and release your mouse button. The clip will slide into place and the edits around it will slide left or right to accommodate. This is what Apple calls the Magnetic Timeline.

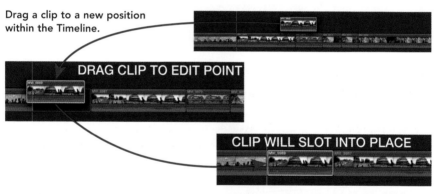

As well as dragging to rearrange, you can also adjust the duration of a clip by clicking to select and then dragging the yellow indicator on the end of the clip in either direction.

Extend/reduce clips by dragging left or right.

You can make the clip shorter from either end, essentially trimming away media, or, if media is available, you can extend the edit from either the beginning or the end, and therefore make it longer. An indicator will display in seconds and frames the change in duration.

It is important to understand the concept of available media. The representation in the Timeline of a clip refers to a media file which exists on the hard drive. Much of the time while editing you will use a  portion of a shot but not the whole shot—there is still media available on the hard drive which can be accessed. If the full duration of the clip has been used, then there is no further media to draw on. You will know when you reach the limit of available media as you will not be able to extend the clip further. The yellow bracket will turn red to indicate that you have run out of media.

Separating Audio from Video

Each clip is made up of video and audio that is locked together. This will be obvious if you have set the clip appearance to Filmstrip view with waveforms visible. To edit to a high level, you need to be able to separate video from audio at will. Any professional editor knows this. Your film needs to be built from the ground up with attention to the soundtrack as well as the picture edit. Picture and sound do not always need to stick together.

Separating audio from video is a fundamental need and enables you to then create a separate sound and picture edit. Sometimes picture and sound need to be locked; sometimes they need to be separated.

1 Click to highlight the clip with which you wish to work.

2 Go to the Clip menu—at the top of the interface, click and scroll to Detach Audio (shortcut: Control/Shift + S).

3 The result will be obvious. Audio, represented in green, now appears separate from video. The Filmstrip view represents the video.

Clip	Modify	View	Window	Help
Create Storyline				⌘G
Synchronize Clips				⌥⌘G
Reference New Parent Clip				
Open in Timeline				
Audition				▶
Show Video Animation				^V
Show Audio Animation				^A
Solo Animation				^⇧V
Show Precision Editor				^E
Expand Audio / Video				^S
Expand Audio Components				^⌥S
Clear Audio/Video Split				
Detach Audio				^⇧S
Break Apart Clip Items				⇧⌘G
Disable				V
Solo				⌥S
Add to Soloed Clips				

One can see clearly that the audio is separated from the video. If you click to select the audio, you can move this independent to the video.

Look to the point where the video and audio are joined. This shows the audio is connected to the video. Whenever you move the video clip, the connected audio will move with it. If you select Audio Only, then you can move this independent of video.

For simple editing leaving video and audio locked together—for more involved editing one needs greater flexibility.

You can also access the audio components, which means the individual tracks of audio.

Choose the Clip menu at the top of the interface and scroll to Expand Audio Components. You will then see the expanded audio tracks for you to access.

Clip	Modify	View	Window	Help
Create Storyline				⌘G
Synchronize Clips				⌥⌘G
Reference New Parent Clip				
Open in Timeline				
Audition				▶
Show Video Animation				^V
Show Audio Animation				^A
Solo Animation				^⇧V
Show Precision Editor				^E
Expand Audio / Video				^S
Expand Audio Components				^⌥S

EXPANDED AUDIO COMPONENTS

Being able to access the individual tracks of audio is important. Most professional cameras will record 2 separate tracks of audio through twin XLRs, and some camera operators will set the camera mic to record to one channel and external mic to the other channel. Being able to mix audio between the tracks and to silence one track while keeping the other track live is essential. This is how most of us have been working for years.

You can expand the Audio Components for clips where audio is combined or for audio which has been detached.

The Concept of Connected Clips

Final Cut Pro X provides several different ways to edit. The first method we discussed is invoked by pressing the letter E. This is called an Append edit—this edits shots onto the end of the Timeline. Therefore, what you are adding to the Timeline does not interfere with existing content in the Timeline.

The next type of edit creates what is called a Connected Clip. The Connect edit places a clip above another clip; it can be seen as a super-impose edit. The uses for Connected Clip will become clear as we get deeper into the editing process. To perform a Connect edit, press the letter Q.

1   Mark a range within a clip within an event. Alternatively, click to select the entire clip.

Either mark the entire clip or a range within the clip.

2   In the Timeline, click to position where you want the edit to take place. I suggest you keep Skimming on. If need be, press S or the icon which toggles Skimming on/off.

Video & Audio   Audio Skimming.
  Skimming.

Note: With Skimming switched on the edit will take place wherever the Skimmer is positioned. With Skimming switched off edits take place wherever the Playhead is positioned.

3   With the Skimmer positioned where you want the edit to take place, press the letter Q.

The clip selected in the Browser is then edited into the Timeline. The result is the clip is positioned one level up from the video which already exists. Notice the clip is attached to the clip beneath it—it is connected.

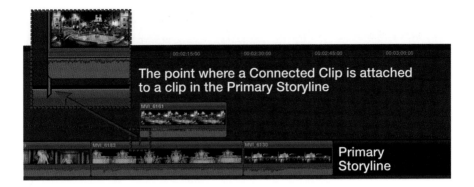

The point where a Connected Clip is attached to a clip in the Primary Storyline

Primary Storyline

Connected Clips are always edited either above or below what is called the Primary Storyline. The Primary Storyline is indicated in a dark shade of gray in the Timeline.

I think of the Primary Storyline as being the main story—this is the hardcore structure of your edit. What you add above as video, and below as audio, is secondary to the main story. It is as if the Primary Storyline is the foundation of your movie, with the rest being built from there.

Connected Clips

4   Edit several Connected Clips into the Timeline.

Click and drag to reposition any of the Connected Clips

5   Click to select a Connected Clip and it can be moved and positioned. If you collide with another Connected Clip, then the clip you are moving will shift up a level, on top of the one it collides with.

Position Connected Clips wherever you wish by dragging.

Connected Clips can be positioned above or below the Primary Storyline. Most often you will see video as Connected Clips above the Primary Storyline, and audio below; however, there is no reason why you can't position video and/or audio above or below the Primary Storyline. They can be dragged to either location.

To move a Connected Clip into the Primary Storyline drag it to the point where two clips meet; then the clip you are positioning will slide into place.

Drag the Connected Clip between two clips in the Primary Storyline.

The clip will then slide into place.

To drag a clip from the Primary Storyline and make it into a Connected Clip simply drag it up or down. This then becomes a Connected Clip and the

gap in the Primary Storyline closes; this is the Magnetic Timeline in action.

Furthermore, when dragging Connected Clips vertically you can prevent the clip from moving horizontally by holding down the Shift key while you drag.

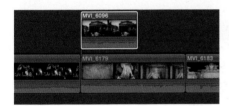

Hold Shift + Drag to move the Connected Clip vertically; this maintains horizontal positioning.

Directing the Flow of Video and Audio

So far we have done two types of edits:

1   The letter E, which is the Append edit; this edits clips directly onto the end of the Timeline.

2   The letter Q, which does a Connected Clip edit above or below the Primary Storyline.

It can be a real problem to do an edit and then have audio competing from two separate tracks. You need to be able to silence audio at will.

There are two ways: first, edit the picture only so the audio doesn't actually get edited into the Timeline; second, once audio has been edited, set the level to zero so that the audio cannot be heard.

Let's start with editing picture only without audio.

In the Toolbar in the middle of the interface, there are three icons which relate to the editing process.

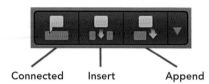

Connected   Insert   Append

These are for:

1   Connected Clip, which we already discussed.

2   Insert, still to be discussed.

3   Append, which we already covered.

The drop-down arrow reveals choices to switch video and/or audio on or off.

Quickly and easily you can choose to edit All (both video and audio) or Video Only or Audio Only.

The ability to channel video and audio separately or together is what is needed to fulfill the needs of the creative process. Since image and sound were first cut together editors throughout the world have been doing the same thing over and over, be it on film, tape, spinning disc, solid state, or whatever the medium may be. The means to achieving results changes with each turn of technology, yet the needs and the essential techniques are the same.

Editing Video Only or Audio Only is the means to achieving the results needed for professional-level work. You can edit the picture over an inter-view and hear the existing soundtrack; you can introduce traffic sound, for example, to cover up an audio join; you can add sound effects, music, narration, or a video cutaway without affecting the soundtrack. This is how editors work.

Notice the shortcuts—embed this in your brain to speed up the process:

- Shift + 1: Video and Audio.
- Shift + 2: Video Only.
- Shift + 3: Audio Only.

You can fly through the editing process directing the edit so only video, audio, or both are edited at will.

Insert Editing

When editing you always have a choice—to push media forward and therefore extend the overall duration of the Timeline, or to add media to the Timeline without affecting the duration (meaning the duration stays the same), that is, the content is edited over existing media.

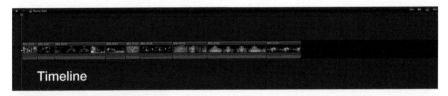

Timeline

A single shot edited as a Connected Clip – the duration remains the same

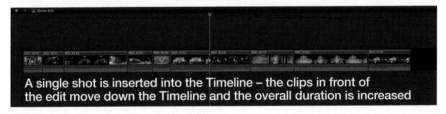

A single shot is inserted into the Timeline – the clips in front of the edit move down the Timeline and the overall duration is increased

Think of it like film—you have a piece of film which you are going to edit to another piece of film. You have a choice: join the film to another piece of film and make the entire edit longer (Insert edit) or take a piece of film out of the existing edit, the exact duration of the film you are adding; thus keeping the overall duration the same (Overwrite or Connected edit).

For the moment, let's concentrate on Insert editing.

1   Select a clip within an event; either choose the entire clip or mark a range.

2   Click in the Timeline where you want the edit to take place.

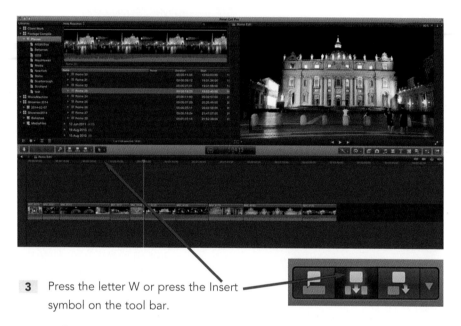

3   Press the letter W or press the Insert symbol on the tool bar.

Notice what takes place: the edit is cut into the Primary Storyline, and all media after the edit is pushed forward. The overall duration of the Timeline has been made longer.

Above: Before the edit.

Above: After the Insert edit—the duration of the Timeline has been increased.

Every time you do an Insert edit that is how it works—it increases overall duration and pushes the clips further down the Timeline away from the edit point.

Overwrite Editing

Overwrite editing is the opposite of Insert editing.

Insert editing makes the Timeline longer and pushes everything forward, whereas Overwrite editing does not affect the duration at all. As the name suggests, using this type of edit writes over a portion of the Timeline.

Use the Edit menu to access Overwrite edit, or use the shortcut, which is the letter D.

Edit	Trim	Mark	Clip	Modify	View
Undo Overwrite					⌘Z
Redo					⇧⌘Z
Cut					⌘X
Copy					⌘C
Paste					⌘V
Reject					⌫
Replace with Gap					⌦
Select All					⌘A
Select Clip					C
Deselect All					⇧⌘A
Paste Attributes...					⇧⌘V
Paste Effects					⌥⌘V
Paste as Connected Clip					⌥V
Duplicate Clip					⌘D
Duplicate Project as Snapshot					⇧⌘D
Keyframes					▶
Connect to Primary Storyline					Q
Insert					W
Append to Storyline					E
Overwrite					D
Source Media					▶

1 Select or mark a Range in a clip within an event.

2 Click in the Timeline and position the Skimmer or Playhead where you want the Overwrite edit to take place.

3 Select to write Video and Audio, Video Only, or Audio Only.

4 Press the letter D or choose Overwrite from the Edit menu.

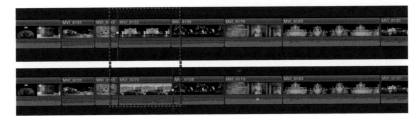

Notice the change to the Timeline where the media has been overwritten, however, the duration of the Timeline remains unchanged.

5 Observe the result: a portion of the content in the Primary Storyline has been written over with media you marked in the Event Viewer.

6 Position the Skimmer in the Timeline and press the space bar to play.

Marking a Range in the Timeline

Just as you can mark a range in the clips in the Event Viewer, you can also mark a range in the Timeline. This lets you define the duration of the content which can be edited into the Timeline, and this applies to the different types of edits such as Connected, Insert, and Overwrite.

A range can be marked in the Timeline in three ways:

1 Click on a clip in the Timeline and the entire clip will then be marked as a Range.

2 Use the letters "i" for in and "o" for out to mark the beginning and end.

3 Alternatively, press the letter R and drag within the Primary Storyline to set the range. A range can also be marked within any of the single Connected Clips.

The duration of the range marked in the Timeline overrides the range marked in any of the clips in the Browser. This means if you mark a two-second range in a clip in an event and then mark four seconds in the Timeline, the four-second duration will apply. If there aren't four seconds of media available then the media which is available will be edited into the Timeline.

While editing, I constantly bounce between the Timeline and Event Library. Points will be marked in the Timeline, something else marked in the Event Viewer. Press Insert, Overwrite or Add to the Timeline as a Connected Clip. Detach the audio and delete the audio. It all happens very quickly.

You need to get into the flow of editing. Processes and technical functions need to become second nature so you hit the keys already lining up in your mind for the next action, constantly reviewing, trimming, adding to, and deleting sound and picture. The ability to mark a range in the Timeline is a very important enabler for achieving precise results.

Editing Overview

So, we have looked at four types of edits:

1. Append: E
2. Connected: Q
3. Insert: W
4. Overwrite: D

The above ways of editing are all incredibly useful for getting content into the Timeline. You can also drag clips directly into the Timeline.

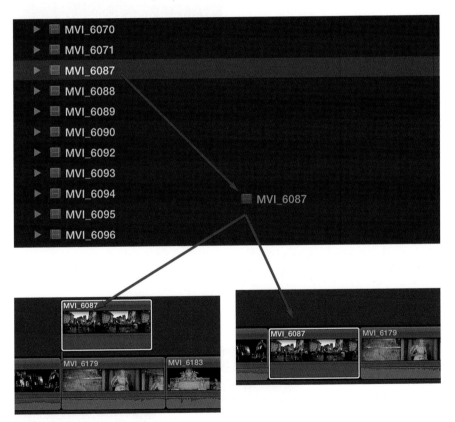

When dragging to the Timeline a Connected edit is performed by dragging above the Primary Storyline; an Insert edit will take place if you drag to the edit point where two clips meet; and a fifth kind of edit is offered if you drag a clip directly on top of a clip in the Primary Storyline—this called a Replace edit.

A contextual menu will appear offering several Replace options. Essentially, a Replace edit means to remove the shot that is already there and replace it with the shot you have chosen.

Replace
Replace from Start
Replace from End
Replace with Retime to Fit
Replace and Add to Audition

The difference between Replace and Overwrite is that Overwrite works to a defined duration, whereas Replace replaces one shot with another with the duration being defined by the shot you are editing into the Timeline. This is unless you choose, Replace with Retime to Fit, in which case the duration will be defined by the original shot, with the shot being edited being either slowed down or sped up to fit in the available space.

You can drag a Connected Clip above or below the Primary Storyline. If the clip is a video clip and you wish for the image to be visible, place the clip above the Primary Storyline. The only likely reason to drag video below the Primary Storyline would be to create a picture-in-picture, or to position a Chroma Key background (dealt with later). If you are dealing with audio it would make perfect sense to drag this below the Primary Storyline as a Connected Clip.

Mentioned earlier, but worth mentioning again, are the key combinations which make this a quick and simple operation.

- Option + 1   Video and Audio
- Option + 2   Video Only
- Option + 3   Audio Only

Remember—it is not only about getting content into the Timeline, it is about defining exactly what is to be edited: Video and Audio, Video Only, or Audio Only.

It should be obvious that Final Cut Pro X has been designed to be efficient and give you results quickly. Hit a few essential key combinations and in no time you have the content in the Timeline to build your film.

Next you need to access Tools, which give you precision to sculpt your edit into a fine-tuned masterpiece.

Editing Tools

There are seven editing tools in Final Cut Pro X which you need to master:

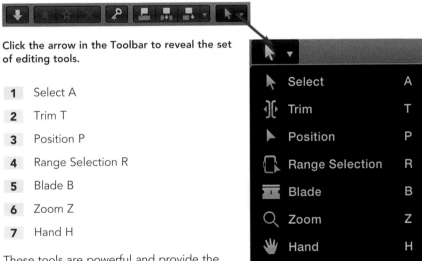

Click the arrow in the Toolbar to reveal the set of editing tools.

1	Select A	
2	Trim T	
3	Position P	
4	Range Selection R	
5	Blade B	
6	Zoom Z	
7	Hand H	

Select	A
Trim	T
Position	P
Range Selection	R
Blade	B
Zoom	Z
Hand	H

These tools are powerful and provide the means to craft your edit. Consider these tools fine-tuning devices in bringing finesse to your edit.

Tools are accessed by selecting the drop-down arrow and then clicking the tool of choice, or you can use the shortcut letters. You can also temporarily select a tool by pressing a letter, for example B for Blade.

The tool is active while the letter is held and then returns to the tool which was last selected when you release the letter.

Select A: This is the home tool. Whatever task you perform with any of the other tools, always return to the Select tool.

Simply press the letter A and the tool is then chosen. The Select tool allows you to pick up clips and rearrange them within the Timeline; you can also move Connected Clips; click with this tool on clips in the Timeline and its abilities become clear.

Position P: Press P and the Position tool is selected. This functions similar to the Select tool with one distinct advantage:

whatever you choose and then reposition in the Primary Storyline overwrites that portion of the Timeline. You are free of the restrictions of the Magnetic Timeline; effectively, selecting the Position tool turns the Magnetic Timeline off, while choosing the Select tool A turns it on. With the Position tool selected, wherever you position a clip, or group of clips, will overwrite that area of the Timeline. If no content exists where you reposition the media, then this space becomes inhabited by the media.

Blade B: Press the letter B to select the Blade tool. This lets you slice through a clip, thereby breaking a clip into smaller

chunks. You can then remove content by pressing the delete key, and the

Below: Highlight a clip or clips in the Timeline.

Below: Delete and clips move to fill the gap.

Below: Hold Shift and press Delete and a gap remains where the media existed.

Magnetic Timeline will then close the gap with the remaining clips; or, you can press Shift + Delete and the content is removed and a gap is left, leaving the duration of the Timeline unchanged. If you press Shift + B, the Blade then becomes a double-blade, enabling you to cut through multiple video or audio layers at the same time.

**Shift + B for
double-blade**

Zoom Z: Expanding and contracting the Timeline are critical to editing in Final Cut Pro X. Sometimes you need to be zoomed

right in on the Timeline for fine detailed work; other times you want to contract the Timeline to get an overview of the edit. Press the letter Z and this selects the Zoom tool. With Zoom selected, you can expand the Timeline by clicking with the magnifier. Where you click is the area that is expanded. Hold the Option key, while zooming, and then you can contract the Timeline. Press Shift + Z to condense the Timeline into the available space.

Hand H: Press the letter H and this gives you the ability to grab hold of the entire Timeline and move it forward or back.

No media is moved when using this tool—it is the visual positioning of the Timeline that is affected. I find the Hand tool useful for manually working on specific areas within the Timeline, particularly when the Timeline is expanded beyond what you can view on the screen.

Range Selection: Lets you quickly and easily define a range. Press the letter R and drag in the Primary Storyline to mark a

range, or within any of the Connected Clips. Also used to adjust audio (described later).

It is important to understand that tools are not used in isolation, they are used in combination with each other. Many times I will use the Select tool to juggle a few shots in the Timeline and then switch to the Zoom tool to zoom in close on a specific area. The Position tool would then be used to move a clip to overwrite another clip, using the Playhead as the point of reference for where the edit is to occur. This brings us to Snapping.

Snapping: This toggles on and off using the letter N. It can also be switched on and off by pressing the icon at the far right of the Timeline.

Snapping N toggles on/off.

When skimming through the Timeline, or when dragging the Scrubber Bar, with Snapping switched on the Skimmer/Scrubber Bar will snap to the edit points.

It is as if the Scrubber Bar and/or Skimmer is magnetically drawn to these—subtle enough that the edit point can be ignored, and strong enough that you can hit the exact point by feeling the hold as you connect to the edit point. This is Snapping.

Very useful. I leave Snapping switched on most of the time. It can also be useful to switch Snapping off so you can freely move through the Timeline without stopping at the edit points.

Snapping on.

Snapping off.

Another way to precisely find your way between edit points is by use of the forward and backward arrow keys. Press the up and down arrow keys and you will skip between edit points. Press the horizontal arrow keys and you move forward or backward, one frame at a time. If you hold Shift + Arrow (forward or backward) you skip forward/backward 10 frames with each press.

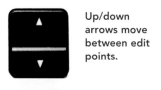

Up/down arrows move between edit points.

Horizontal arrows move forward a frame at a time; hold Shift + Arrow and move 10 frames at a time.

Between Snapping and the arrow keys I find myself able to precisely locate any point in the Timeline, quickly and accurately.

Turning Skimming On and Off

The letter S toggles Skimming on and off.

Shift + S toggles audio on/off while skimming.

Skimming   Skimming + Audio

Simply drag across media in the Events Browser or Timeline and the results will be obvious.

Skimming is a great feature for reviewing the footage in your Timeline and clips in the Events Browser, however, there are times when it can get in the way.

Therefore, it can be very useful to hit the letter S and switch Skimming off momentarily, or even for extended periods, while you then use the Scrubber Bar to work your way through the Timeline. Often, while editing, I will hover over the letter S, switching Skimming on/off as needed.

The Concept of Storylines

I've mentioned the Primary Storyline. Just to recap, this is indicated in the Timeline with a dark gray strip; everything else in the Timeline connects or becomes part of the Primary Storyline. The Primary Storyline is where the main action happens—it is where the movie is built. This does not diminish the importance of content which is secondary to the Primary Storyline. The point is that the bulk of editing takes place either in or connected to the Primary Storyline.

Every time you do an Insert edit, an Overwrite, or an Append edit, the result is then added to the Primary Storyline.

When you do a Connect edit (shortcut Q) the result is added to a Secondary Storyline (above or below the Primary Storyline).

Connected Clips are the ones which appear outside the Primary Storyline.

You can also create Secondary Storylines. Simply highlight one or more Connected Clips in the Timeline, and choose Create Storyline.

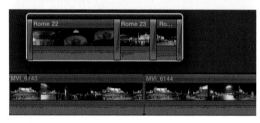

A Storyline is defined by a darker gray border around the clips. Dissolves can now be added between clips and the Storyline can be moved as a single unit.

Using the Select tool click and move the Secondary Storyline wherever you want it to be placed.

Why would you want to create a Secondary Storyline? There are several reasons:

1   A Storyline can be moved as a complete unit. It is much easier to move several clips together as a Storyline than as individual Connected Clips because as a Storyline they all move together. Just as Connected Clips are anchored to the Primary Storyline, so are Secondary Storylines. Secondary Storylines always connect to the Primary Storyline.

2   You can add dissolves or other transitions to the clips inside of a Storyline, whereas it is not possible to add dissolves and other transitions to Connected Clips. Be aware that clips which are combined into a  Storyline will then have the same abilities, in terms of editing techniques that exist in the Primary Storyline.

The rules inside a Secondary Storyline are the same as in the Primary Storyline. The Magnetic Timeline works the same, and each of the tools performs the same function.

If you wish to return clips from being inside a Storyline back into Connected Clips, then highlight and drag the clips out of the Storyline. They will connect to the Primary Storyline where you release them.

Alternatively, drag clips out of a Secondary Storyline and into the Primary Storyline. These will then be inserted into the Primary Storyline at the edit point closest to where you release them.

Trimming (in general)

There are several ways to trim media in the Timeline. A basic way to trim is to take the Blade tool, B, cut a clip in the Timeline, and then highlight and delete the media where you have cut. Working this way, if you press the Delete key the media will be removed and the rest of the Timeline will move to fill the

Blade

Shift + B for double-blade.

space. If you press Shift + Delete, then a gap will be left equivalent to the media which has been removed.

You can also trim, using the Select tool, A, by dragging the edit points.

Hover over an edit point and the tools above are revealed: you can drag to extend or reduce clip durations in either direction according to available media.

Hover over an edit point, on either side where two clips meet, and notice that a tool appears with two opposite-facing arrows. There is small filmstrip down the bottom; indicators show which way the tool will operate. If you drag one way you can lengthen or extend the shot you have selected. You can do this from the beginning or end of the shot. The limits to how far you can extend the shot depend on how much media is available on the hard drive.

As you drag to extend or reduce the duration on either side of the edit point, the Viewer shows a visual indication of the outgoing and incoming frame.

Providing you have switched on Show

Timeline: ☑ Show detailed trimming feedback

Detailed Trimming Feedback in Preferences, a twin monitor display in the Viewer will visually show the changing edit point.

These two methods enable you to trim in a primitive way: you can slice with the blade, or you can drag the end or beginning point of an edit to lengthen or shorten a shot. These techniques are basic and effective.

For more refined editing, you need to access the Trim tool.

Working with the Trim Tool

Press the letter T to select the Trim tool. This gives you more controls with which to work. With this tool you can perform Roll, Slip, and Slide edits.

⫴ Trim   T

Roll edits: Press T to select the Trim tool. Click at an edit point between two clips. Drag the Trim tool from side to side and you see the edit point can be rolled in either direction according to available media. An indicator will show in seconds and frames changes to shot duration. When rolling edits, the shot is extended on one side and simultaneously reduced on the other side.

Press T to select the Trim tool.

The edit can be rolled left or right according to available media.

If you have detached audio from video it will be clear how useful this is.

Above: Video has been rolled to the right of the audio, creating a split edit. This provides an effective way to offset video and audio.

You can conveniently roll an edit point without affecting the duration of the Timeline. Audio, if detached from video, is unaffected by Roll editing.

As you trim the results are reflected in the viewer.

As you trim, the Viewer will show the outgoing and incoming frames of the edit (provided you have switched on Show Detailed Trimming Feedback in Preferences). This applies to all functions in Trim mode.

Slip edits: A Slip edit affects the portion of the clip which exists in the Timeline. While slipping the edit, adjusting the start and end point, you draw on the original media, which needs to be longer than the portion included in the Timeline for this type of edit to work. You adjust the clip within the confines of the existing duration.

Press T to choose the Trim Tool. Place your cursor in the center of a clip and drag the clip in either direction within the Timeline. According to available media, the clip content will then be adjusted; as you drag a visual display is shown of the outgoing and incoming frames (you need to make sure you have Show Detailed Trimming Feedback selected in Preferences).

Press T and click in the center of the clip.

Detailed trimming feedback is displayed as you drag.

Drag right or left to move the media within the confines of clip duration.

Slide Edits

Press the Option key with the Trim tool selected and click in the center of a clip in the Timeline. You can move the selected clip in the Timeline left or right, extending or reducing those clips on either side of the edit, at the

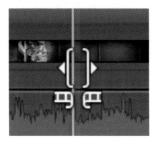

Press T and the Trim tool appears as above.

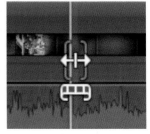

Press T and hold down the Option key to be able to perform Slide edits.

same time maintaining the duration of the edit you are moving. This gives you the means to reposition a clip within those on either side of it. The result is the clip you slide will eat into the clip on one side and extend the media from the other.

Clip in original position.

Drag to the left—notice the duration of the clip is unchanged, however, the clip on the left has been made shorter while the clip on the right has been made longer.

Drag to the right—the clip to the left is extended. The red indicates all available media has been used.

Note: This edit relies on surplus media on hard drive to be available from the clips on either side of the edit. If the Slide edit doesn't work, reduce the length of the clips on either side of the clip you are sliding and this will create available media to work with.

It may not be immediately clear how useful all these trimming methods are. Let me say, without doubt, if you only use one of the techniques described above, learn how to

perform Roll edits. This is as simple as pressing T to select the Trim tool, and then dragging the edit point to a new position. One side of the edit is extended while the edit on the opposite side is made shorter. I think of it as being like a giant film reel releasing film on one side and winding it onto the take-up spool on the opposite side. This lets you precisely adjust edit points while watching the visual feedback to show incoming and outgoing points. Furthermore, if you are working with audio separated from video, you can roll the edits for video without affecting the audio, which lets you do all sorts of magic in the editing.

The Precision Editor

This is a fantastic device which lets you quickly view available media and then adjust the clips on either side of the edit point. It is used for fine-tuning your edits.

1   Press A for the Select tool.

2   Double-click on an edit point in the Timeline.

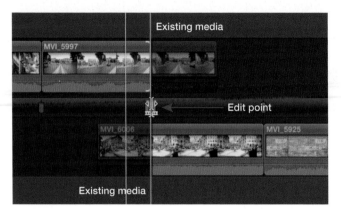

The Precision Editor will now open, and you can see the existing media beyond the edit point, on either side, as being darkened. This media is referred to as "handles". It exists on the hard drive and you can draw on this media to extend the edit if you wish.

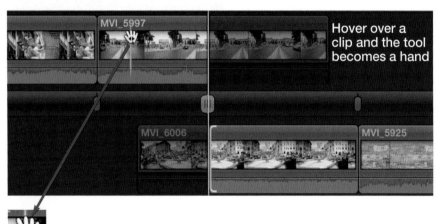

3   If you hover your cursor over one of the clips within the Precision Editor, the icon becomes a hand. You can use the hand to adjust the edit point by dragging. Note: this does affect the duration of the Timeline.

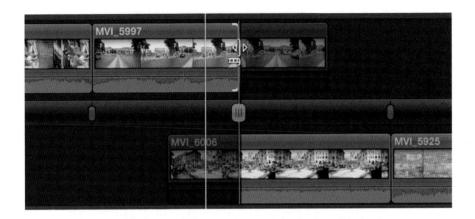

4. If you click on the edit point you can move the media by clicking or dragging to extend or reduce. Again, this will affect the duration of the edit.

5. You can also drag the center indicator and this will adjust the edit point without affecting the duration, essentially performing the same function as a Roll edit.

Note: If you separate video and audio, then you can move the edit point as described in point 5 and audio will remain unaffected.

In summary, within the Precision Editor you have three separate modes with which to fine tune your edit:

1. Use the hand to extend or reduce the media.

2. Click the media and extend as a range.

3. Move the center indicator to perform the same function as a Roll edit.

Hand

Click Media

Center Indicator

Experiment with these methods and it will become clear what the uses are.

To close a clip back to the normal collapsed-state, choose the Close Precision Editor button (bottom right of the Timeline) or double-click the Select tool A on the edit point and the Precision Editor disappears.

Trimming While Playing Back in the Timeline

One final way to trim media, this time while playing back in the Timeline. You can trim a clip which is stationary or "on the fly" while playing back your edit.

- Option +]   Trim end of current clip.
- Option + [Trim beginning of current clip.

Press Option +] The trim will take place where the Playhead is positioned. Note the difference in the Timeline below. The media forward of the trim point moves to close the gap.

Media moves back to close the gap.

Press Option + [The trim will take place where the Scrubber Bar is positioned. Media preceding the Scrubber Bar moves forward to close the gap and the duration of the Timeline is reduced.

Media moves forward to close the gap.

By hitting the above key combinations, media is then cut from the end or the beginning of the clip where you are currently positioned. Media in the Timeline moves to close the gap and the duration of the Timeline is affected.

If you have audio separated from video, then different rules apply:

- Option +]   Video is trimmed, audio is not (audio detached).
- Option + [Video is trimmed, audio is not (audio detached).

Option +] Video is trimmed, audio is not (above).

Media moves back to close the gap and note, below, the audio from the trimmed clip continues beyond the trimmed video.

Option + [Video is trimmed, audio is not.

Note: The audio now precedes the trim point.

Retiming

Retiming is the word used in Final Cut Pro to describe fast or slow motion.

The controls for slow retiming read Slow 50%, 25%, and 10%, and the Fast controls are for 2x, 4x, 8x, and 20x. Don't be deceived that these are limiting—you can have any speed you want!

1 Mark "in" and "out" points or highlight the clip you wish to adjust.

2 Choose the Retiming menu from the Toolbar. Apply the Slow or Fast setting of your choice.

3 Observe in the Timeline that a color indicator has been applied showing the speed as a percentage. The color blue is used to represent fast motion; orange for slow motion.

Drag the right end of the Retiming slider and the indicator will show precise speed changes as you drag. You can adjust the speed to the exact duration you require.

If you wish to reset back to 100% click the speed controls in the center of the clip and set to normal 100%.

Or choose Reset Speed from the drop-down menu under the Speed Control icon.

For best quality slow motion choose the Modify menu, choose Retime, Video Quality, Optical Flow. This is very simple to achieve and is accessed through the Retiming controls, or under the Modify menu at the top of the Final Cut Pro X interface.

Rendering will take longer with Optical Flow switched on but the payback in terms of quality is worth it.

Choose Hide Retime Editor to hide the controls in the Timeline

You can also choose to Ramp the speed which means the speed will vary incrementally from 100% to 0% or vice versa. Experiment with the controls as there is a lot on offer to work with.

Create a Freeze Frame

This is easy and is found in the Retime Controls.

1   Click on a clip in the Timeline and park the Playhead on the frame you wish to freeze. Press the Retime button.

2   Choose the Edit Menu—scroll to Add Freeze Frame (Shortcut Option + F). The result is a freeze frame added to the point in the Timeline you defined. By default the freeze is 4 seconds. This is set in Edit Preferences.

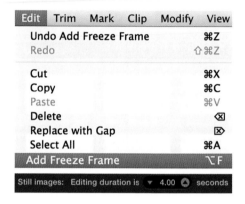

You can also create a freeze frame by parking the Playhead on a clip in the Timeline—then choose the Retime menu and scroll to Hold. A freeze is then created at this point in the Timeline—if you drag the end of where it reads zero per cent you can then increase or decrease the duration of the freeze.

You can then use the Blade to cut the freeze into smaller pieces and reposition as you wish.

Setting Clip Durations

You can easily change the duration of any of the shots in the Timeline.

1 Click to select a shot in the Timeline.

2 Choose the Modify menu and scroll to Change Duration (Control D).

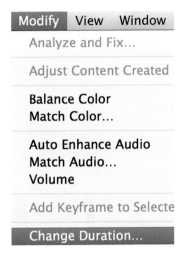

3 Notice the center of the Toolbar is lit up in blue showing the current duration.

4 Type a new duration, for example for 5 seconds, type 500 followed by the Return key.

The new duration is applied to the clip. If you are making the duration shorter this will be applied, however, the maximum amount you can extend a clip is the amount of media that exists on the hard drive.

Setting the duration of the clip is versatile in that it does what it says, which is to set a clip to a predetermined duration; it also offers a quick way to check the duration of any clip in the Timeline. Just highlight a clip, press Control + D, and the duration is displayed in front of you.

Solo Clips

When the Timeline gets busy and crowded with a lot going on, it can be incredibly useful to only listen to the audio from a specific clip or a few select clips and to mute everything else.

Solo button toggles on or off.

This is easily achieved by highlighting a clip or several clips and pressing the Solo button. This is located top right of the Timeline interface, and appears as an icon of the letter S wearing headphones (shortcut Option + S).

1 Highlight the clip you wish to solo.

2 Press the Solo button.

Yellow on. Gray off.

When a clip is solo you will only hear the audio of that clip and all the other clips are silent. This is indicated visually; all the other clips are grayed out.

You can selectively solo multiple clips if you wish.

Soloing can be particularly useful when working with multiple sound elements. You may have voice over, sound effects, and music. To combine all these elements you need to be able to adjust these independently to create a complete soundtrack, with cohesive elements that don't fight against each other. When creating the audio soundtrack soloing is a powerful means to isolate a particular part of the soundtrack and adjust as needed

Disable Clips

You can also disable clips, which means to kill the audio and video from a particular clip or clips.

1 Using the Select A tool highlight a clip or group of clips in the Timeline.

2 Choose the Clip menu and scroll to Disable or press the letter V.

Clip	Modify	View	Window	Help
Create Storyline				⌘G
Synchronize Clips				⌥⌘G
Reference New Parent Clip				
Disable				V

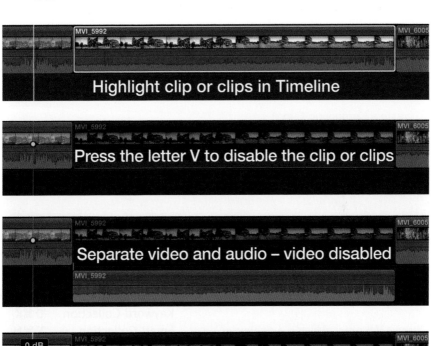

Highlight clip or clips in Timeline

Press the letter V to disable the clip or clips

Separate video and audio – video disabled

Separate video and audio – both disabled

The clip or clips you have disabled remain in the Timeline, however they cannot be seen or heard.

It is very easy and quick to at any point press the letter V and disable a clip and then press V to enable it again. When you are working with multiple layers this can be very useful.

Compound Clips

We've covered several concepts so far: the Events Library, Keywording, Connected Clips, and Primary and Secondary Storylines. Now, it is time for one more concept: Compound Clips.

Essentially, a Compound Clip is several clips, or even an entire Timeline of media, collapsed down into a single clip. The single clip is the Compound Clip.

Compound Clips can be expanded so that you can go back inside to access the media, which makes up the Compound Clip. If you wish, you can lose the Compound Clip entirely and return to the original expanded state of the media by choosing Break Apart Clip Items.

To create a Compound Clip:

1 Highlight the clips in the Timeline which you wish to combine into a single clip.

2 Choose New Compound Clip from the File menu at the top of the interface or press the shortcut, Option + G.

Observe the result, which is a single clip in the Timeline of the duration of all the highlighted clips which previously existed.

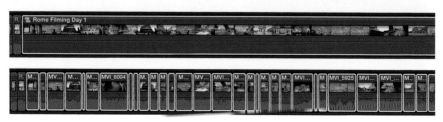

| Clip | Modify | View | Window | Help |

Create Storyline	⌘G
Synchronize Clips	⌥⌘G
Reference New Parent Clip	
Open in Timeline	

| **Audition** | ▶ |

Show Video Animation	^V
Show Audio Animation	^A
Solo Animation	^⇧V

| **Show Precision Editor** | ^E |

Expand Audio / Video	^S
Expand Audio Components	^⌥S
Clear Audio/Video Split	
Detach Audio	^⇧S
Break Apart Clip Items	⇧⌘G

| **Disable** | V |

Choose Break Apart Clip Items to turn a Compound Clip into each of its individual components.

Double-click anywhere on the Compound Clip and you can see the individual clips; these can be adjusted, recut, and changed as you wish, and the changes are then reflected when playing back the Compound Clip.

To return to the Timeline, with the Compound Clip in position, click the arrow back button located top left of the Timeline.

To get rid of a Compound Clip so that the original, expanded media appears in the Timeline, highlight the Compound Clip and choose Break Apart Clip Items from the Clip menu (shortcut Command + Shift + G). This will return you to the edited clips and the Compound Clip will no longer be visible.

The huge advantage of working with Compound Clips is you can take a very busy, sophisticated edit, and reduce its size so that it is manageable. Too much information in the Timeline can be unwieldy to work with—to collapse it can make life simpler. A warning: don't overuse Compound Clips and don't put Compound Clips inside of Compound Clips. This has been known to stress out the computer!

Whizzing around the Timeline Using Markers

It can be useful to use Markers to pinpoint a location to which you can quickly return. A Marker can be left as a signpost anywhere in the Timeline, they can be color coded, and notes can be assigned to them.

1   Park the Skimmer anywhere in Timeline and press the letter M. This will leave a marker on the clip where you were positioned in the Timeline.

2   Go somewhere else in the Timeline and again press the letter **M**.

3   One more time repeat the process.

Markers in blue

You should now have the Timeline with three separate Markers. You can move between the markers by pressing the following key combinations:

- Control + '   Jump forward to next marker.
- Control + ;   Jump backward to previous marker.

This is incredibly useful—it means at any time you can jump to a predetermined point in the Timeline. It is very simple to quickly move backwards or forwards.

Markers serve more purposes than simply to move around in the Timeline.

When setting a marker, instead of pressing M, press the letter M twice in quick succession. A dialog box will open, giving you the choice to enter details for the marker.

To do item in Red.

If you press Make to Do Item the marker will then visually stand out in the color red. This is easy to spot, even on a very busy Timeline.

If you control-click on a Marker you get options to choose from. Notably, you can cut a Marker, to get rid of it, or mark as a To Do Item. Once you have completed a To Do Marker check the Completed Box and the To Do item will now turn green.

If you press Shift + M while positioned on a Marker, or double-click a Marker, this will reveal the notes which have been entered.

I think of markers as being like pegs or beacons—you can home in very quickly exactly where you want to be.

There are three types of Markers: Marker, To Do and Chapter. Chapter Markers are used in DVD authoring, To Do are temporary indicators for work still to be completed, and Markers are general purpose locators to take you to a specific place in the Timeline.

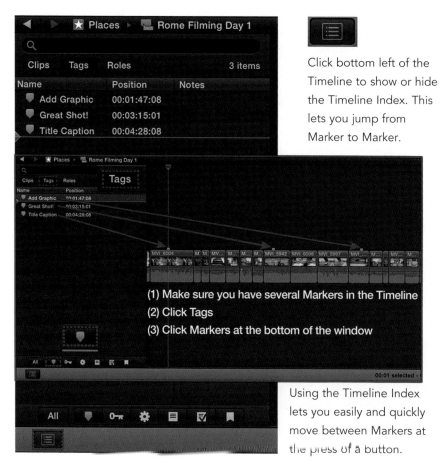

Click bottom left of the Timeline to show or hide the Timeline Index. This lets you jump from Marker to Marker.

(1) Make sure you have several Markers in the Timeline
(2) Click Tags
(3) Click Markers at the bottom of the window

Using the Timeline Index lets you easily and quickly move between Markers at the press of a button.

Reveal All the Clips Used in Your Project

If you want to see a quick overview of the media you have used in your project, meaning a complete listing of all the clips, then click the lower left of the Timeline on the Timeline Index icon—the list of clips will now appear in front of you.

 Click this icon, located bottom left of the Timeline, to reveal the Timeline Index.

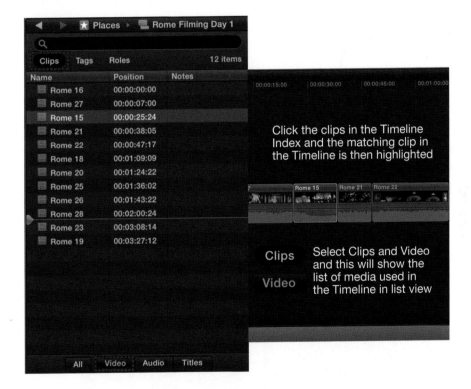

You can use the arrows to move up or down or click any of the clips to show in the Viewer; note as you click the selected clip is then highlighted in the Timeline.

Control-click the clip in the Timeline and select Reveal in the Event Browser to locate and/or match a frame to a clip (Shortcut Shift +F).

Locating Clips in the Event Library or on the Hard Drive

When I worked in online edit suites, filled with open-reel tape machines, spinning in sync, with an edit controller and vision mixer to make it all happen, we used to do a fair bit of match frame editing. This meant you would mark the "in" point on a source tape, and the exact frame would be spooled to on the original master tape. It was the quickest way to locate the original media and also very useful in effects creation.

In Final Cut Pro X, you have two facilities to help you track down media and to do a match frame edit if you wish. Control-click any clip in the Timeline and choose one of the following:

1. Control-click any clip in the Timeline. A menu will appear—scroll to Reveal in Browser.

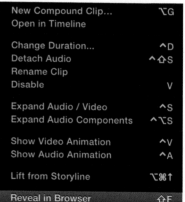

2   Control-click the Clip in the Event
Browser and choose Reveal in Finder.
This will now show where the clip is
located on hard drive.

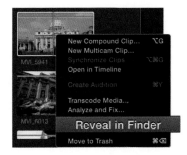

Both of the above are incredibly useful for
tracking down your media within the project or
on the drive, and enabling you to match the
frame edit if you need to.

Cut, Copy, and Paste

Any of the media in the Timeline can be cut, copied, or pasted, just like using a
word processor. Clips can be copied and pasted within a project or between
different projects.

- Command + X   Cut
- Command + C   Copy
- Command + V   Paste
- Option + V   Paste as Connected Clip

1   Highlight any clip or clips you wish to cut or copy.

2   Press Command + X to cut the clips or Command + C to copy the clips.

3   Reposition the Skimmer or click to position the Scrubber Bar and press
Command + V. The media will then be pasted at the place you have
decided.

4   If you wish to Paste as a
Connected Clip then type
Option + V. This clip is then
positioned above for video,
or below for audio.

Connected Clips pasted into the Timeline

Note: When cutting from the Primary Storyline the clips to the right will move
and close any gaps which have been created (the Timeline will be made shorter);
when pasting into the Timeline the result is that of an Insert edit: any media after
the Insert will be shunted down the Timeline to the right, and the Timeline will
therefore increase in length. When pasting as Connected Clips the duration of
the Timeline will remain unaffected.

Show Used Media and Show Unused Media

A fantastic feature, added to Final Cut Pro X 10.1, is the ability to Show Used Media. What this means is any media which has been edited into a project, is then displayed in the Events Viewer with an orange line to indicate which media has been used.

Go to the View menu and switch on Show Used Media Ranges. This is a toggle—to turn off select Hide Used Media Ranges.

View	Window	Help
Playback		
Browser		
Hide Clip Names		
Show Waveforms		
Hide Marked Ranges		
Show Used Media Ranges		
Show Skimmer Info		

Hide Used Media Ranges

As you edit content into the Timeline you will see an orange line through each of the clips in the Event Library which have been used. The orange line is specific to the portion of media which has been used.

MVI_6768   MVI_6776   MVI_6779   MVI_6780   MVI_6781

Orange bars represent Used Media in filmstrip view.

This is particularly useful as the editor can quickly see which media has not been used within an Event or Keyword Collection.

When editing, we are always looking for the best shots which we have not used. The process involves continually reaching into the reservoir of shots and extracting the best of the best, and compiling this in order to make a specific visual statement. By continually being able to see what media has been used is a big advantage.

Furthermore, you can also show only unused media within the Event Browser if you press Control + U. To return the Browser to the default setting, click in the upper left corner of the Browser and select All Clips.

Choose all clips top left of Browser.

Automatic Backups of Libraries, Events and Projects

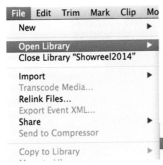

While you are editing with Final Cut Pro X the software saves a copy of the Library, and all the Projects and Events within the Library, every 15 minutes. This can be a lifesaver if you need to go back in time to a previous version of an edit. You can choose from the available list, which is time stamped.

1 Highlight the Library you wish to open the Back up for.

2 Choose File—Open Library—From Backup.

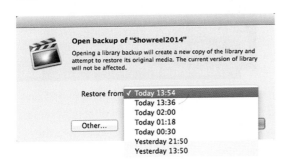

The list of backups for that Library will now be in front of you.

125

3 Click the Backup you wish to open and select Open.

A new copy of the Library will now be created, which is Timestamped, while the Library you had been working with also remains open.

The copy of the Library which has been created is stored, on hard drive in the same location as the Library from which it was created.

Note: You can manually set the location for where the Backup files will be stored if you wish, though I tend to leave the settings at the default. By default the backups are stored in the User Movies folder on your boot hard drive.

Versioning

While accessing the Library Backups is great to return to a previous version of the entire Library, it can be advantageous to duplicate your project while working to create a copy or version of the project to work with.

Control-click on a Project and access either of the commands:

(i)   Duplicate Project.

(ii) Duplicate Project as Snapshot.

The commands are very similar and either will create a duplicate of your project. The

difference being, if you use Compound Clips or Multicam Clips in more that one project—changes to the Compound or Multicam Clips will then affect the same Compound or Multicam Clips used within other Projects. This applies with the first command Duplicate Project.

By choosing Duplicate Project as Snapshot effectively grabs a moment in time; any changes to Compound or Multicam Clips will not affect other projects.

For myself—I usually choose Duplicate Project as Snapshot with the knowledge that this creates an independent duplicate to work with.

Whichever method you choose note that the duplicate will be Timestamped giving you the information as to when that particular version was created.

Creating Custom Project Sizes

Not all content that is created is widescreen or standard aspect ratio. Sometimes unusual format sizes are required for conference venues, advertising, video walls, or vertical portrait monitors.

You need knowledge of the format and frame size you are going to be working with.

1 Choose File—New—Project.

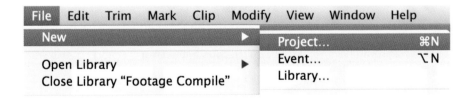

2 Choose Custom Size in Video Properties.

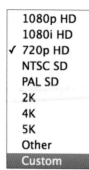

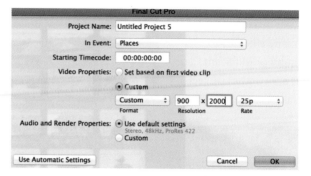

3 Key in values for image size and frame rate.

4 Press OK. You can now edit footage into the Timeline at the custom size which you have set.

Square   Vertical

Extreme widescreen/cinema

You can create square, vertical or extreme widescreen using custom setting. By adjusting the Transform controls you can then reframe the image within the custom frame you have set. More on Transform in the Effects chapter of this book!

Transform
Controls

Active Clip Indicator

As you have been editing you may have noticed the little white ball which appears within a clip as you work. This is known as the Active Clip Indicator and serves as a reference to show you where you are positioned within the Timeline.

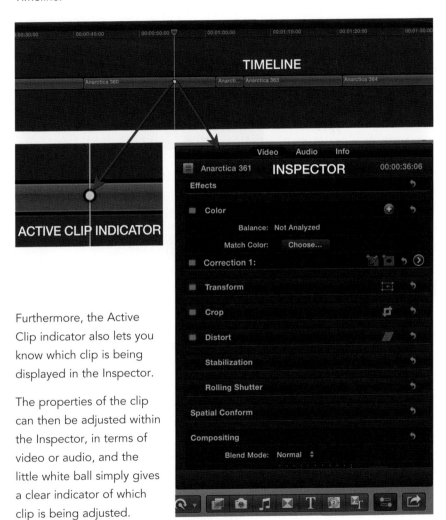

Furthermore, the Active Clip indicator also lets you know which clip is being displayed in the Inspector.

The properties of the clip can then be adjusted within the Inspector, in terms of video or audio, and the little white ball simply gives a clear indicator of which clip is being adjusted.

Auditioning

Auditioning gives you the means to quickly switch between different shots in the Timeline. I think of it as being like a giant carousel switching sources in real time though a giant projector . . .

1 Highlight a clip or range in the Timeline.

2 Highlight a clip or clips in the Event Browser.

3 Drag the clips from the Event Browser on top of the clip in the Timeline wherever you choose and then select Add to Audition.

Alternatively, choose from the Clip menu at the top of the interface.

Notice a new spotlight icon appears to the left top of the clip to show that clips are ready to be Auditioned.

4 Press the letter Y to open the audition, or control-click on the clip and select this command.

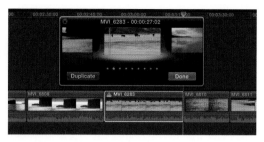

The Audition window will open in front of you. Position the Playhead and press the space bar to play.

Press Control + forward/back arrows to skip through the shots you have lined up in the Audition window.

When you find a shot you want included in the edit, press Done and the clip will drop into place.

Done

If you want to add another clip or clips to the audition choose Add to Audition and continue the process. You can remove a clip from the Audition by selecting it and pressing the Delete key. Once you are done Control-click on the Audition and choose Finalize Audition.

Add to Audition

Finalize Audition

Rendering

Rendering is the process which takes place to build the frames of your movie for output. Rendering is not always required, however, when footage is manipulated and changed, then it does need to be rendered, not necessarily to play back, but for final output. Changes such as color correction, opacity changes, retiming, and stretching or cropping of the image, or adding titles, all require rendering.

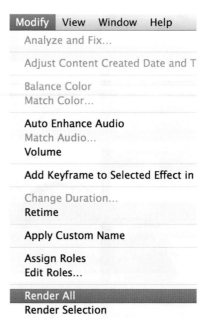

Modify	View	Window	Help

Analyze and Fix...

Adjust Content Created Date and T

Balance Color
Match Color...

Auto Enhance Audio
Match Audio...
Volume

Add Keyframe to Selected Effect in

Change Duration...
Retime

Apply Custom Name

Assign Roles
Edit Roles...

Render All
Render Selection

Whenever you see an orange bar at the top of the Timeline this means that the portion of media needs to be rendered.

If you have Background Render switched on in Preferences, then rendering will begin within a few seconds. Final Cut waits for a lull in activity and then rendering kicks in . . .

If you have Background switched off then you can manually start the render process by choosing the Modify menu and scrolling to:

- Render All:
  Control + Shift + R
- Render Selection:
  Shortcut Control + R

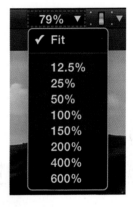

Much of the time I work with Background Rendering switched off in Preferences and manually render when I choose. This is useful for two reasons: (1) rendered files take up hard drive space, therefore avoiding rendering saves generating unnecessary render files (2) having Background Render fire up every time you stop for a few seconds can be distracting.

Adjusting represented size of image in Viewer

Most of the time you are editing you should keep the display of the images set to Fit into the available viewing area.

1 Click the percentage symbol, top right of the Viewer.

2 Select Fit.

This fits the image into the available space for viewing. It can be advantageous to increase or decrease the size of the represented image for compositing work. This will be covered later in the Effects chapter.

Switching between Better Quality & Better Performance

A very useful command, found under Viewer Display Options—top right of the Viewer—is the ability to change the display resolution of the images as they are played back.

Essentially you can either choose Better Quality or Better Performance.

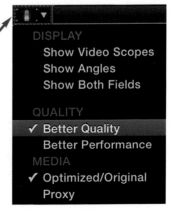

1 Click Viewer Display Options—top right of the Viewer.

2 Select Better Quality or Better Performance.

In an ideal world one would always work with Better Quality set, however, depending on the processing power of your Mac, the drives you are using, the amount of memory and which graphics card is Installed in the machine—all these factors affect the ability of the system to playback the video content smoothly. Beyond that, and of huge importance, is the codec you are working with. Final Cut Pro X will work with many different codecs natively: all flavours of ProRes, XDCAM EX, DVCPro HD, DV, AVCHD—however, how well it plays back content native in those formats depends on the factors already mentioned.

I switch between Better Quality and Better Performance many times during the editing process. When I need to view something at full quality Better Quality is the choice—even if the playback is not perfectly smooth. For general editing, Better Performance can be the most suitable choice.

For best performance you may choose to render any unrendered content in the Timeline. However, many editors choose not to render and to work with the real time playback abilities of Final Cut Pro X. By choosing Better Performance rather than Better Quality often unrendered material will play back in real time.

Control + R—render range or highlighted clips in Timeline.

Command Shift + R—render everything in the Timeline.

Other times, to view at full resolution, simply render the portion of the Timeline you wish to view and then you will get full resolution and smooth playback when choosing Better Quality.

Working with Proxies

Right at the beginning of this book, in the Preferences, I discussed the idea of working with low resolution Proxy files. These files—the Proxies can be generated by Final Cut Pro X

There are 2 ways to do this:

(i) Set preferences to automatically generate Proxies on import. Then, each time you import media, by default Proxies will be generated.

(ii) Manually instruct Final Cut Pro X to generate Proxies once the media has been imported.

To manually transcode media to Proxy:

1 Highlight the media in the Event Library—if you wish to transcode all the media within the Library select all (Command + A).

2 Control click the Media and choose Transcode Media.

3 Choose Create Proxy.

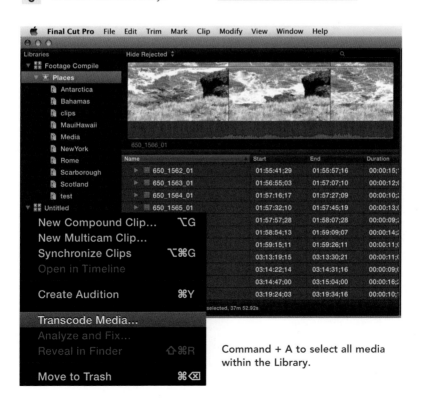

Command + A to select all media within the Library.

Click the Dashboard (center of the interface) and the background tasks taking place will be revealed. Click the arrow next to Transcoding and Analysis to see what processes are taking place.

Note: The indicator in the Dashboard showing processing taking place.

Click the Dashboard to reveal Background Tasks.

The Proxies are an exact duplicate of the master media, at lower resolution, which means editing is quicker, smoother and snappier. Real time performance is better and rendering speeds along much faster than it would with the full resolution media.

The downside is the lower quality of the represented image. However at any time you can switch to full resolution with a simple command.

While editing, to switch between full resolution Optimized/Original Media and Proxy—choose Viewer Display Options—top right of the Viewer and then select either option: Optimized/Original or Proxy.

You can then choose to edit as Proxy (low resolution) or Optimized/ Original (high resolution). The obvious method would be to do all the editing as Proxy and then when it

comes to outputting, switch to
Optimized/Original. This is important as
if you do not set to Optimized/Original
the output file will be encoded at Proxy
resolution! Not very good if you are
generating a master file.

Note: If at any time you
see a red Missing Proxy
indicator in the Event

Browser, Viewer or Timeline, this means the Proxies have not been generated or
have somehow become offline. The solution—generate the Proxies or switch to
Optimized/Original media.

Multicam editing

There are two ways to cut between multiple camera sources. The most efficient
way, in terms of time, is to cut live. This requires each of the cameras to be
plugged into a vision switcher which is then used to mix the program in real
time.

The output of the vision switcher is then recorded or broadcast live.

The other way is to do it in postproduction using editing software such as Final
Cut Pro X. The implementation of Multicam in Final Cut is the best I have seen.
The process is reliable, streamlined, and offers power which simply isn't found
in other systems.

The success of your Multicam edit begins during the filming, well before you
get into the edit suite.

Be aware—shooting multi camera is going to generate a lot of content.
This in turn will use up a significant amount of hard drive space. If you shoot an
hour performance, using three cameras, you will end up with 3 hours of footage.
If you shoot for an hour on four separate cameras you will acquire four hours of
footage. And this doesn't include render material while editing, and masters
which are output. Multicam takes up space and processing power.

In Final Cut Pro X you can then edit this footage native—depending on how powerful your computer is and which codec has been recorded—or, you can convert the camera footage into Proxies, enabling Final Cut Pro X to deal with this at low resolution, before you then switch to full resolution for output.

Transcoding: ☐ Create optimized media
☑ Create proxy media

You can also set Final Cut Pro X, within Playback preferences, to Create Optimized media. This means, if the original codec is difficult to work with, Final Cut Pro X will then convert the footage to ProRes for editing.

Playback: ☑ Create optimized media for multicam clips

Creating a Multicam Clip

1. Organize the media you wish to work with using Multicam. I suggest you create a Library and within a single Event put the camera originals. Ideally all cameras will have been left running during recording, so there is only a single start and stop for each record. Each camera should have audio— even camera mic—of the live record.

GWC12_CAM-B_1222

Name	Start
▼ 8 Mar 2014 (4)	
▦ 158_1702U01_1	03:50:54:24
▦ 477_0748_1	22:32:05:11
▦ BRITTA 0070U01_1	01:27:33:00
▦ GWC12_CAM-B_1222	12:48:29:23

2   Highlight the media you wish combine into a Multicam Clip.

3   Control click any of the highlighted clips—a contextual menu will appear. Choose Create Multicam Clip.

4   A window will now open. You need to enter a name for the Multicam Clip and define the Event where this will be stored. By default, this will be the Event where the clips you are combining are stored.

You can choose Use Audio for synchronization—and the software will then match the audio for each clip and then combine into a Multicam clip. This is an easy and effective method, providing you have continuous audio of decent quality for each of the clips.

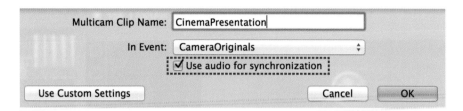

If you don't have continuous audio then you need to venture into Custom Settings and choose Angle Synchronization. Here sync clips by the First Marker on the Angle.

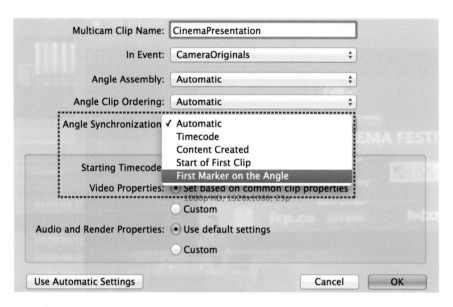

To manually sync by Start of First Clip or First Marker on the Angle, will require some preparation in advance before you get to the stage of creating a Multicam Clip.

By far the easiest method is to Use audio for synchronization.

☑ **Use audio for synchronization**

Synchronizing Multicam Clip

Synchronizing Angles

5 Wait while the computer checks though each of the clips and combines the different angles into a single clip—this is the Multicam clip. This process can take some time.

6 Once the Multicam clip has been created edit this into a Project in the same way as you would any other clip. To see the different angles you need to open what is called the Angle Viewer.

Shortcut to Angle Viewer: Shift + Command +7

7 Select the Window Menu—scroll to Viewer Display—Show Angles.

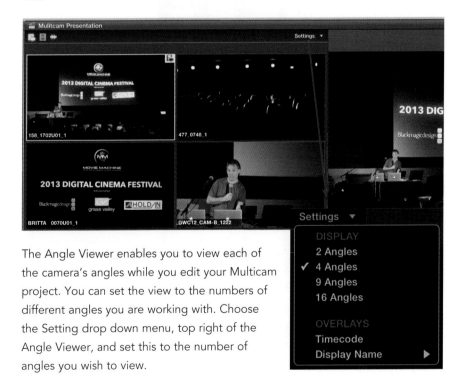

The Angle Viewer enables you to view each of the camera's angles while you edit your Multicam project. You can set the view to the numbers of different angles you are working with. Choose the Setting drop down menu, top right of the Angle Viewer, and set this to the number of angles you wish to view.

Editing Multicam Clips

Multicam Clips work just like any other clip in Final Cut Pro X—the big difference being that contained within each Multicam clip are each of the angles for you to work with. I think of Multicam Clips as being similar to Compound Clips in that several clips are combined together to create a single clip—the Multicam Clip.

▼ 8 Mar 2014 (5)	
158_1702U01_1	03:50:54:24
477_0748_1	22:32:05:11
BRITTA 0070U01_1	01:27:33:00
CinemaPresentation	01:27:33:00
GWC12_CAM-B_1222	12:48:29:23

CinemaPresentation

Multicam clips are represented by 4 squares.

When it comes to editing the Multicam Clip the process is straightforward.

1 Edit the Multicam Clip into a Project.

Multicam clip in Timeline defined by 4 squares next to clip title

158_1702U01_1

2 Open the Angle Viewer (Shift +Command+7)—and press Space Bar to play the content. If everything has synced correctly you will see the video and audio running together. If everything is not in sync you need to revisit the process of creating the Multicam Clip.

3   Look to the controls at the top of the Angle Viewer. You can choose to edit both audio and video, video only, or audio only. My method is to establish the best audio track, do an audio only cut of the best audio right at the beginning of the Timeline, and then select to edit video only.

Video & Audio   Video   Audio

4   Now open the Angle Viewer. Position the Playhead on the Multicam Clip and press the Space Bar to play. As the video plays click on the camera angle of choice in Angle Viewer and each edit will be recorded. Alternatively press the numbers on your keyboard—1, 2, 3 and 4 for the corresponding angle and you can cut your content live, just like you are operating a vision switcher in a TV studio control room.

The cuts in the Timeline represent the changes in camera angles.

5   Play back your edit. You can now refine this using the trim tools. Select T for trim, and then slide the edit points and adjust as you wish. As the audio is continuous the audio remains unaffected.

6 Should you wish to manipulate the audio separate to the video you can choose to Detach the audio in the Multicam clip (choose Clip—Detach Audio.)

Detached audio is moved independent of audio using the Trim tool.

Audio is detached and video is moved independent of audio using the Trim tool.

There is another area that needs to be investigated and this is the Angle Editor. You enter the Angle Editor by double clicking anywhere on the Multicam Clip— or by Control clicking on the Multicam Clip and choosing Open in Angle Editor.

Double click the Multicam Clip in the Timeline to enter the Angle Editor or Control Click the Multicam Clip and select Open in Angle Editor.

The Angle Editor shows all of the clips which make up your Multicam Clip. The names on the clips above don't mean a great deal, however, I could have manually numbered this as Camera 1, Camera 2, Camera 3 and Camera 4.

In the Angle Editor click to select angle, this will make it live, you can then adjust the color and other attributes in the Inspector. The changes you make will then apply to all use of that angle within the Multicam edit. You can also adjust the audio levels—the levels you set will then boost or lower the volume of that angle within the Multicam edit.

Select the audio icon to make this track live. This is for monitoring purposes. Set the level and this will then adjust the audio from this angle accordingly when cut to in the Multicam clip within the project.

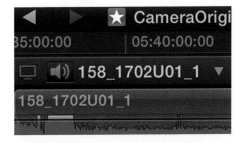

Set the audio level by dragging the black line up or down.

Click the video symbol and you can adjust attributes about the video which will then appear in the Multicam Clip within the project.

For example, select the angle in the Angle Editor, adjust the color correction in the Inspector, and the results will then appear in the Multicam Clip within the Project.

To exit the Angle Editor, click the arrow back—top left of the Timeline window. You can then continue editing your Multicam project. Any changes you made within the Angle Editor will now be included within your edit. As mentioned, this could be changes to color correction of a particular angle or angles, changes to audio, you could add effects, and you can even include other angles and content within the Multicam Clip.

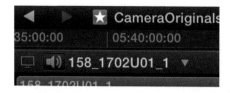

Select Clips in Angle

Sync to Monitoring Angle...
Sync Angle to Monitoring Angle

Set Monitoring Angle
✓ Monitor Audio

Add Angle
Delete Angle

For example, you could create additional angles within the Angle Editor and drag content into this angle which you have created. Once the content is positioned within the angle—you can reposition and fine-tune as you wish in relation to the other existing angles. This could be tremendously useful when adding graphics to a presentation which has been recorded live. Furthermore, if you need to adjust any of the other Angles within the Angle Editor, click these to make the Angle live, and then drag the content to reposition as you wish. Be careful not to mess up the sync of items already in place!

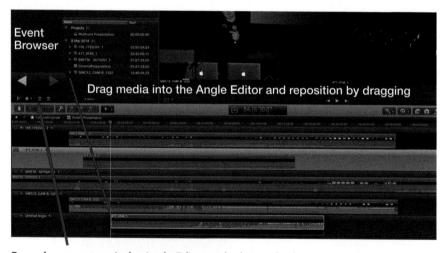

Drag media into the Angle Editor and reposition by dragging

Press the arrow to exit the Angle Editor and take you back to your Multicam edit.

This has been a quick overview of Multicam in Final Cut Pro X. This is tremendously powerful and effective. For many years I worked as a live director in television, cutting programs live to air. The implementation of Multicam in Final Cut Pro X is, without doubt, sophisticated and brilliantly thought-out. This software lets us do things we could have only dreamed of a few years ago . . .

Copying media between Libraries and Events

At any time you can drag media from Library to Library or Event to Event.

Highlight media contained within a Library—if you click and drag the media from one Event to another, the media is moved. This is to say that it will be removed from the original Event and placed into the second Event. If you want to leave the media in the original Event, and, at the same time, move to another Event, hold down the Option key and this will copy the media to the second Event while leaving the media at its original location.

Note the Plus sign to indicate that the 3 clips will be copied to the new location and also remain in the location from where they were dragged.

If you are working with media located on an external drive, then the links will be copied—in other words the media will be referenced to. You will get a warning to alert you to this.

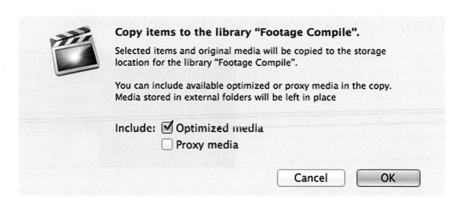

You can choose to create Optimized and/or Proxy Media. Each time you move media between Events in different Libraries you get this message.

If you edit content between Libraries then the media will be copied, or, if you are working with external media then the links will be copied.

You are editing clips between libraries.
Clips and media will be copied to the library "Footage Compile". Media stored in external folders will be left in place.

At any time you can locate the original media on hard drive by control clicking on a clip and choose Reveal in the Finder.

Furthermore, you can see the contents of a Library bundle by Control Clicking on the Library bundle and choosing Open Package Contents.

From the Finder, you can check the size of a Library to get an indication of how much media is stored within it.

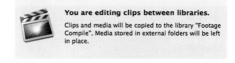

New Compound Clip...   ⌥G
New Multicam Clip...
Synchronize Clips   ⌥⌘G
Open in Timeline
Create Audition   ⌘Y
Transcode Media...
Analyze and Fix...
Reveal in Finder   ⇧⌘R
Move to Trash   ⌘⌫

Highlight the Library and press Command + I. This will reveal information about the Library bundle. Even Proxies, which are low resolution, can add considerably to the size of the Library.

⊖ ○ ○ 🎬 Footage Compile Info	⊖ ○ ○ 🎬 DedoInterviews Info
Footage Compile 2.81 GB	**DedoInterviews** 116.24 GB
Modified: Today 22:20	Modified: Today 23:39

The size of the Library will vary depending if the media is internal or external, and whether or not Proxies have been used.

If you wish to look inside the Library bundle to see what is contained inside of it—Control Click on the Library bundle and choose Open Package Contents.

The contents will be revealed and you can then open up the folders within the Bundle to see what media resides there. You can also see which media is referenced to as these appear as Aliases which link to the original media.

These Aliases point to the original media which is stored external to the Library.

Beware! Apple did not intend for users to be messing about in this area and you can damage or destroy the Library and all the Projects within it—or you could potentially delete media! There aren't too many reasons why you need to go into this area so the best advice is to steer clear!

Organizing media in the Event Browser with Folders

By now you are well familiar with Libraries, Events and Projects—and how to edit content from Events into the Timeline.

When things get crowded in the Event Browser with many different Keyword collections it can be useful to file these away inside of Folders.

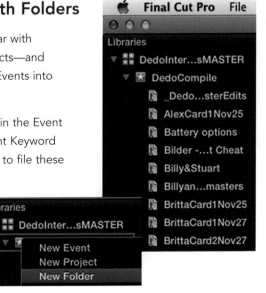

1 To create a Folder choose the File Menu—choose New—Folder. Alternatively, Control Click on an Event and choose New Folder (shortcut Shift+Command+N).

2 Name the Folder.

3 You can then drag Keyword collections into the Folder.

4 Create as many Folders as you wish inside of any Event. You can even group Folders inside of Folders.

The result is you can collapse a complicated unorganized structure into categories so you can locate just what you need. Between Keywords and Folders, and all the other organizational abilities in Final Cut Pro X, we have a powerful way to organize and retrieve our media.

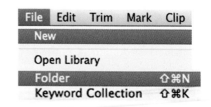

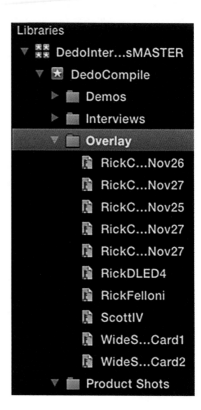

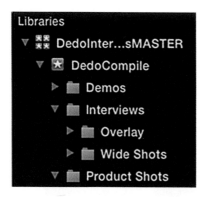

Putting it all Together

Just remember editing isn't one thing, it's everything; it is how you use the tools in combination with each other which will let you fly through the editing process and turn out the results.

There is still a huge amount to explore with Final Cut Pro X. For the moment, absorb the key concepts of how to organize media, how to get footage edited into the Timeline, and how to make it work in terms of pace and structure. Next we move on to audio production, where you make your production sound as good as it looks.

AUDIO

| 00:02:50:00 | 00:03:00:00 | 00:03:10:00 | 00:03:20:00 | 00: |

00:02:47:06

100
%

HR   MIN   SEC   FR

slandFerry1997 14   StatonIslandFerry1997 15

slandFerry1997 14   StatonIslandFerry1997 15

Sound Mixing

Even though this is a separate chapter in the book, I want to make the point that sound mixing is not necessarily something which happens separate from the rest of the editing. I will mix sound as I cut picture. Sometimes, if I have the time, I'll spend more time on the audio, which may well be after the picture edit is complete. Sometimes, when there is no time, I may call on some of the audio-functionality built into Final Cut Pro X to sort out any of the differences in levels between clips.

I'm old school. I like manual control over my audio so I know what is going on. However, I'm also on the cutting edge. I like to make use of new technology to better the end product and to make my life easier. Final Cut Pro X has some nice facilities to help you create a seamless audio mix.

The basics which one must run through, in terms of audio production, for producing any video or film include the following processes: (i) adjust audio levels (ii) add sound fades (iii) mix the sound to be music, narration, sound effects, or whatever (iv) balance any peaks or falls in the sound and check the output level (v) work with stereo pairs (vi) build multiple layers of audio and solo/disable audio at will (vii) synchronize audio, where a master record needs one or more cameras to be synced together (viii) keyframe audio fades, and (ix) pan tracks.

That's enough for now. There could be more work beyond this, but the list above is pretty comprehensive in terms of the general tasks which need to be fulfilled.

Back to Basics

Just a reminder, clips inside Final Cut Pro X appear as video and audio combined in the same clip. By running through the options in Clip Appearance you can view only the audio information if you choose, or you have the option to show video thumbnails and audio combined.

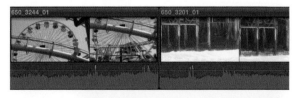

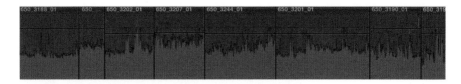

For the purpose of mixing sound, it can be useful to make the audio as large as possible by adjusting the clip height.

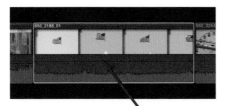

Double-click here to collapse

Double-click the audio to separate visually.

You can view separate video and audio by double-clicking the audio track to visually separate the two.

Clip	Modify	View	Window	Help
Create Storyline				⌘G
Synchronize Clips				⌥⌘G
Reference New Parent Clip				
Open in Timeline				
Audition				▶
Show Video Animation				^V
Show Audio Animation				^A
Solo Animation				^⇧V
Show Precision Editor				^E
Expand Audio / Video				^S
Expand Audio Components				^⌥S
Clear Audio/Video Split				
Detach Audio				^⇧S
Break Apart Clip Items				⇧⌘G

If you want to separate video and audio so that they are truly separate, highlight a clip and choose Detach Audio from the Clip menu.

The audio then becomes a Connected Clip to the video. Therefore, if the video is moved, the audio, which is connected to the video,

will move with it. However, you also have the power to move the audio

Audio moved separate to video

separate from the video just by clicking on it and dragging. If you wish to combine video and audio into a single clip, then highlight the elements and choose Compound Clip from the File menu.

For those who have used other editors, the familiar way to work with audio is to have two

tracks to access. Most professional cameras record to two separate audio tracks, with separate XLR inputs; some even allow for four separate tracks.

It is important to be able to access those tracks inside of Final Cut Pro X.

It is as simple as Control-clicking on the audio and selecting Expand Audio Components or the Clip menu and scroll to Expand Audio Components.

Adjust the Audio Level within a Clip

The basic job of adjusting audio levels from clip to clip is as simple as can be in Final Cut Pro X.

Make sure you have Clip Appearance set so that you can clearly see the audio waveforms. When mixing audio, I will often set the display to only show the audio waveform (the first choice in Clip Appearance).

Switch on the audio meters so you can visually see the changes in the audio level.

Press the Audio Meters icon in the Dashboard to show or hide the meters.

Audio meters

Green, during playback, shows the audio is good, yellow shows you are peaking, and red shows you are over-peaking and risk distortion.

The basic rule is don't hit the red on the meters. I let my audio run at between –12 and –6 dB.

If you wish to make the audio display even larger, drag the Clip Height slider to increase or decrease the size.

Adjusting audio levels within a clip is simple:

1. Use the Select Tool A and drag the black line in the center of the clip up or down.

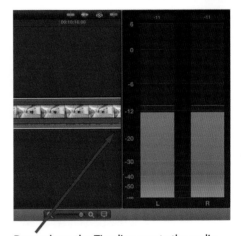

Drag where the Timeline meets the audio meters to extend the width.

2. You will notice indicators in audio clips in the Timeline. Drag the black line in the clip up, raising the volume; when you release, the indicators will show yellow or red to indicate over-peaking. Adjust so the absolute peaks hit the yellow but not the red.

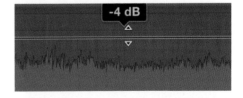

An indicator will show in dB how much you raise or lower the audio.

3. Check the playback on the audio meters to confirm these are correct.

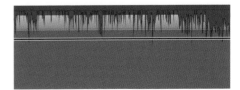

You can also raise the audio level in small increments, on the fly during playback, by pressing **Control +** (volume up) or **Control –** (volume down). Simply highlight the clip and adjust the level as you listen to the result, again watching the audio meters as well as the clip indicators.

Fading Audio

The audio fade has been with us forever and is the primary way of smoothing out bumps in the audio so you can create a montage of sound which blends seamlessly together. Sometimes you want an audio cut, sometimes you want a fade. A fade provides a gentle transition.

The audio can be faded very easily from the head or the tail:

1 Position your curser over a clip in the Timeline.

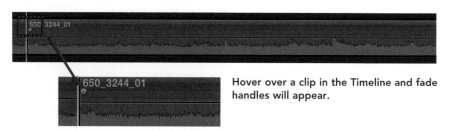

Hover over a clip in the Timeline and fade handles will appear.

2 Hover your curser over a clip in the Timeline. Look to the ends of the clip and notice at the beginning or end of the clip are handles, represented by a small dot.

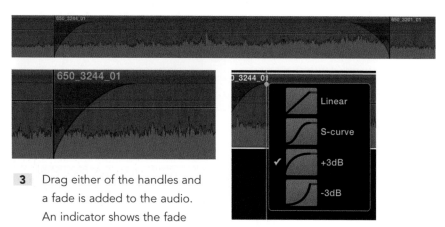

3 Drag either of the handles and a fade is added to the audio. An indicator shows the fade duration as you drag.

If you Control-click on the handle at the beginning or end of the shot, you are given options to change the shape of the fade. Experiment with these and listen to the result and choose that which is most suitable.

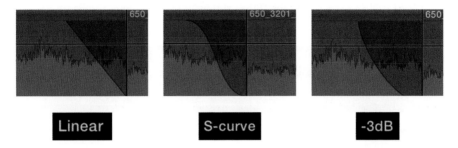

Linear   S-curve   -3dB

Fading Audio Using the Range Tool

You can also fade the audio within a clip using the Range Tool R. This provides an incredibly useful means to making fine adjustments to the audio within a single clip.

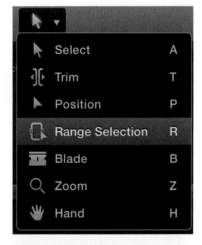

Select   A

Trim   T

Position   P

Range Selection R

Blade   B

Zoom   Z

Hand   H

1   Press the letter R to select the Range tool or choose the drop down menu in the Toolbar.

2   Click with the Range tool and drag within a clip in the Timeline to define the area you wish to adjust.

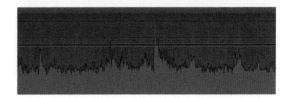

3   Once you have marked the range, click the black line in the center of the clip and drag this up to

increase the audio level or drag down to reduce. An indicator will show the level of increase or decrease in dB as you drag. The result is that a fade is added to the beginning and end of the range. You can see the fade represented visually; furthermore, you can adjust the fade points by dragging.

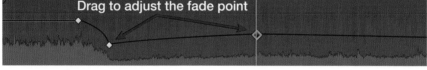

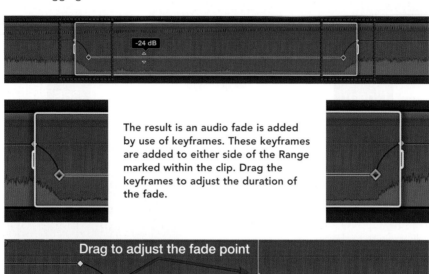

The result is an audio fade is added by use of keyframes. These keyframes are added to either side of the Range marked within the clip. Drag the keyframes to adjust the duration of the fade.

Drag to adjust the fade point

Keyframing Audio

To Keyframe means to change over time. You can plot points within the audio of a clip and make adjustments as you wish by dragging the fade points.

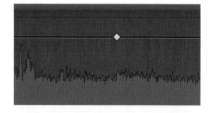

1   Hold down the Option key and click the black line within a clip. Notice a dot will be added to represent an audio Keyframe.

Control + Click the black line in the centre of the clip to add audio Keyframes

Repeat the process. Option + click to add as many points as you wish.

2 Grab any of the audio Keyframes and drag to adjust. You will visually see the fades plotted within the clip with an indicator showing the increase or decrease in dB.

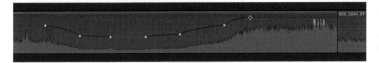

3 Listen to hear the result, and watch the audio meters to confirm you don't over-modulate.

To remove any of the Keyframe points you have added, click the Keyframe point, which will then turn orange and press Delete on your keyboard. Press shift and click to highlight multiple Keyframe points—these can be then be moved together in the Timeline by dragging.

Adding Audio Mixes

Along with the audio fade there is the audio mix, which is an overlapping fade between the two audio sources. This is one of the most used tools for creating a smooth-sounding mix. A quick audio fade, two or three frames, can be used to remove pops and clean up edits, whereas a longer audio fade can be used to introduce sounds to the mix so that nothing is jarring. When mixing audio, most of the time, the goal is not to alert the viewer to the mix; rather, it should be unnoticeable. Using audio fades can help us achieve this.

We can mix between two audio sources. To do this, we need at least two clips edited side-by-side in the Timeline with overlap, meaning more media must exist on the hard drive to draw upon to produce the fade. You can actually check available media by opening the Precision Editor. Double-click the edit point and available media, beyond that which has been used, appears transparent. Note: You cannot detach audio once the Precision Editor is open. This needs to be done first.

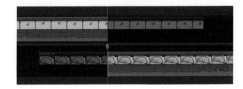

1   Make sure you have two clips cut together with audio detached.

2   With the Select A tool chosen, drag the audio from one of the clips toward the clip next to it. The clip which you are dragging toward will then shunt out of the way (it is important that the Select A tool is being used!).

3 Drag the Fade Handles for the incoming and outgoing clips. Visual indicators show the duration of the fade as you drag. You can therefore quite easily plot an 8-frame or 12-frame audio fade. For precise control, expand the Timeline using the Zoom tool, Z; you can zoom right down to the subframe level if you wish! Play back and listen to confirm the result is what you want. You may also wish to Roll the video to follow or precede the audio transition.

Expand Audio Components

There are several ways you can access the individual tracks recorded on location. As mentioned earlier, most professional cameras record two tracks of separate audio via XLR jacks.

Choosing to Expand Audio Components is a quick way to expand the individual audio tracks. You can then adjust the levels on each of the tracks, the pan controls, and apply audio effects. Once adjustments have been made you can select Collapse Audio Components and, once again, a single stereo pair will represent the two audio tracks. Any changes you have made while the audio components are open continue to take effect once the audio components have been collapsed.

You can Expand Audio Components with audio which has been detached and also with audio which is combined into a single clip with the video.

1 Control-click on a clip in the Timeline—choose Expand Audio Components. Alternatively choose the Clip menu and scroll to Expand Audio Components.

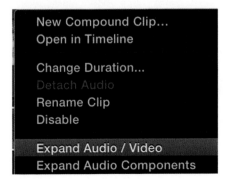

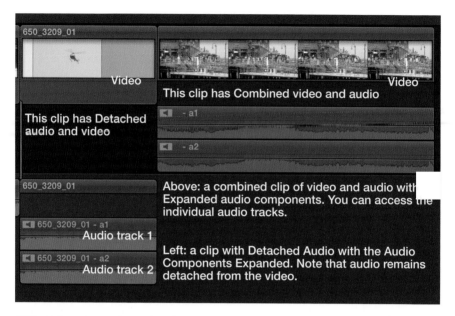

650_3209_01

Video

This clip has Combined video and audio

Video

This clip has Detached audio and video

- a1

- a2

650_3209_01

Above: a combined clip of video and audio with Expanded audio components. You can access the individual audio tracks.

650_3209_01 - a1

Audio track 1

650_3209_01 - a2

Audio track 2

Left: a clip with Detached Audio with the Audio Components Expanded. Note that audio remains detached from the video.

2   Adjust the audio within the individual audio tracks as you wish. The same rules apply for adding fades or adjusting audio levels, as with audio in clips which have not had the components expanded.

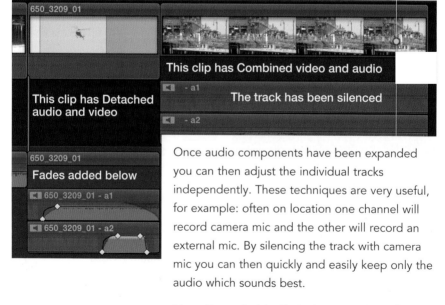

650_3209_01

This clip has Combined video and audio

This clip has Detached audio and video

- a1

The track has been silenced

- a2

650_3209_01

Fades added below

650_3209_01 - a1

650_3209_01 - a2

Once audio components have been expanded you can then adjust the individual tracks independently. These techniques are very useful, for example: often on location one channel will record camera mic and the other will record an external mic. By silencing the track with camera mic you can then quickly and easily keep only the audio which sounds best.

Note: Expanded Audio is shown in Blue, whereas Detached Audio is represented by Green.

Break Apart Clip Items

Another way to reveal the separate audio tracks is to choose the command Break Apart Clip Items. This will Detach Audio from video and break the audio into separate tracks.

You can select multiple clips in the Timeline and then select Break Apart Clip Items and the dual tracks are then available to access for each of the clips.

1 Highlight the clips in the Timeline you wish to work with.

Clip	Modify	View	Window	Help
Create Storyline				⌘G
Synchronize Clips				⌥⌘G
Reference New Parent Clip				
Open in Timeline				
Audition				▶
Show Video Animation				^V
Show Audio Animation				^A
Solo Animation				^⇧V
Show Precision Editor				^E
Expand Audio / Video				^S
Expand Audio Components				^⌥S
Clear Audio/Video Split				
Detach Audio				^⇧S
Break Apart Clip Items				⇧⌘G

2 Choose the menu Clip at the top of the interface and scroll to Break Apart Clip Items (shortcut: Shift + Command + G). You can then add fades and adjust the levels as you wish.

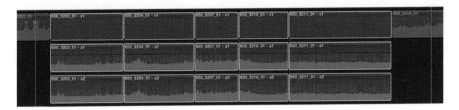

The result is each of the audio items become independent Connected Clips with the video remaining as the main clip in the Primary Storyline. You can therefore move audio separate to video—or if you move video the connected audio clips will then move with it. You can also choose to move single audio clips separate to everything else. These audio clips now function as connected clips and therefore the rules of working with Connected Clips apply.

You need to be careful not to lose sync—which is easy to do when moving audio independent of video.

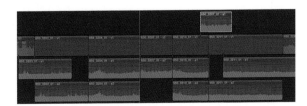

Relationship of the Inspector to Audio Output

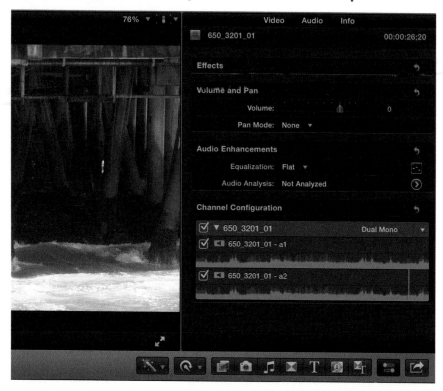

A key part of the interface which we have barely touched upon so far is the Inspector.

The Inspector can be accessed by pressing the Inspector symbol (right of the interface).

The shortcut Command + 4 will toggle the Inspector on or off.

The Inspector is a place where you can access many of the controls for editing, audio editing, effects production, and titling. The Inspector reacts to the clip you have selected; therefore, click the audio of a clip and Inspector displays the audio properties and choices. Choose the video and you can access controls which affect the video. Once we get onto effects production, you will see controls and parameters specific to this area.

Click the audio of a clip in the Timeline and open up the Inspector window; press the Inspector icon on the interface or choose Command + F4.

Setting Audio Pan Controls

The first video editing I ever did was working in a two-machine Betacam suite. Two-tape machines wired up, a player, and a recorder with an edit controller to control each of the machines. There was a Preview button and a Record button bang in the center. This was standard Beta, analogue half-inch tape, before Beta SP and way before DigiBeta hit the scene.

On Betacam, you could work with two tracks of audio: stereo, left or right. You could do a lot with two tracks—music on one, interview on the other, then do a mixdown to add some effects. It was primitive, but it worked, and we knocked out results which were broadcast every night on the six o'clock news, onlined in two-machine suites and fed out to the world.

In that two-machine suite was an audio mixer, so we could ride the levels and mix the audio live. At the top of the mixer were pan controls. It had the essential knobs—turn one way and audio could be directed to the left or the right channel, turn the other and you could balance the audio so that the master track fed equally to tracks 1 and 2 on the record machine.

That's what pan controls do. This lets you mix audio evenly so the track you have chosen will play out of both the left and right channels, or, you can choose to direct the sound left or right or anything in between. This is the process by which the editor creates a stereo or mono mix.

It is important to be aware when setting the pan controls in Final Cut Pro X that you can work with audio where video and audio are represented as a single clip or you can work where the video and audio are Detached.

Furthermore, you can choose to work with the clip as two separate tracks, by using the Expand Audio Components command. You can then apply the pan controls to the individual tracks.

To set the audio pan controls in Final Cut Pro X:

1   Click on a clip in the Timeline.

2   Open the Inspector (Command + 4 to toggle on and off).

3   Click the second tab, Audio.

4 You can now choose a pan mode.

5 Choose Stereo Left/Right.

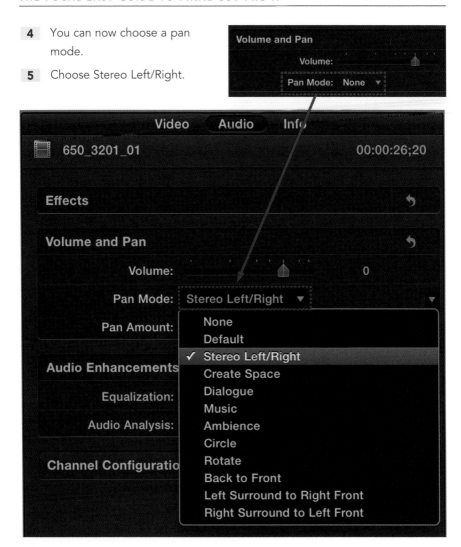

6 Use the slider to adjust the pan amount. Using this you can adjust the pan Left/Right and you can hear the result as you pan.

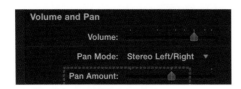

Drag the Pan Amount slider one way and you hear the audio out of the left speaker; drag the other way and sound comes from the right. Set the Pan control in the middle and sound is distributed equally through both speakers. The result is also reflected on the audio meters (press the Meters icon on the Dashboard in the Toolbar if these are not visible).

3 Be aware adjusting the pan for a single track of stereo audio is very different

Press to reveal audio meters.

from adjusting the pan for individual tracks of audio. That is when you use Expand Audio Components, or Break Apart Clip Items; this will then let you access the individual tracks. I like to know the makeup of the audio tracks and much of the time I choose to work with dual audio tracks. I can quickly remove stray audio or camera mic by deleting a track or by silencing the audio. The best audio can then, if I choose, be panned to mono so the sound is equally heard out of the two speakers.

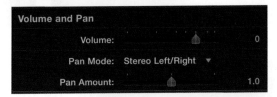

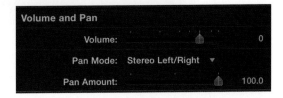

As mentioned earlier, adjusting pan controls was standard practice in edit suites over twenty years ago in broadcast tape suites. It gives you the means to control your audio, to produce a stereo or mono mix, and to get rid of unwanted sound.

Switching Audio Tracks On and Off in the Inspector

Audio tracks can be turned on or off in the Inspector simply by checking or unchecking the controls.

1 Click on a clip in the Timeline.

2 Look to the Inspector under the Audio tab. Notice at the bottom is an area called Channel Configuration—click the disclosure triangle to reveal the audio associated with the clip. This can be set to dual mono or stereo. Think of the representation in Channel Configuration, within the Inspector, as being a reflection of the audio in the Timeline.

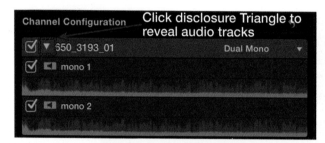

Above: Dual mono representation of the clip in the Inspector.

Left: Tracks can be muted by checking or unchecking the box to the left. This presents a quick way to silence the audio.

Left: If the Channel Configuration is changed to stereo, then the result is that one Track of audio, not two, is then visible in Channel Configuration.

Boosting Audio Levels with the Gain Filter

Many times audio is recorded on location at a lower level than is ideal. This can be fixed in the edit suite by boosting the audio. The means to adjust audio in the Timeline is limited to a maximum of +12 dB. When you need more volume, do the following:

1 Highlight the clip you wish to adjust in the Timeline. If you are working with separate video and audio, then highlight the audio.

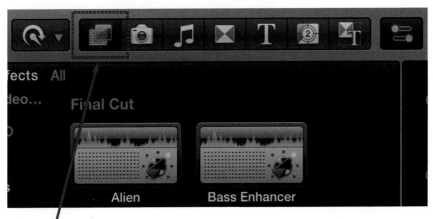

2 Open up Video and Audio Effects.

3 Scroll down so you can see the audio choices and click Levels.

4 Locate the Gain filter. You then need to apply this to the clip you have highlighted by double-clicking the Gain icon or by dragging this onto the clip.

Drag the Gain filter onto audio in the Timeline.

Drag the Gain filter onto audio in the Timeline.

The Effects window for audio and video is a pane which shows available effects, separated with video at the top and audio at the bottom.

Note the search dialog box at the bottom of the window. Key in the name of an effect, such as Gain, and the search results will be shown before you.

Once you learn the name of the effects you use most frequently you can then key in the info to find them very quickly.

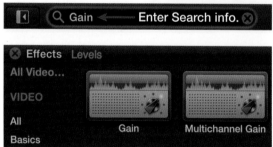

The search results are then displayed before you.

5 Once you have applied the Gain filter to a clip go to the Inspector, look to the audio controls, and under Effects is Gain. Click the arrow to reveal adjustable parameters and functionality.

6 Adjust the parameters. You can boost the overall volume considerably and you have other controls, including Pan control, and the ability to mono the track or swap channels.

Drag the slider to increase or decrease the gain. Maximum gain is + 24 dB, plus you can increase audio in the Timeline by + 12 dB.

Keep an eye on the audio meters, particularly when boosting with Gain, as it is easy to completely over do it.

Using the Gain filter provides a quick way to increase the audio level. If you need even more level, then apply the Gain filter twice or as many times as you need to boost the audio to whatever level is required.

Once the effect is applied you can play your audio and adjust in real time to hear the result.

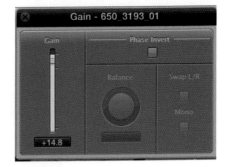

You can adjust the parameters within the Gain controls.

Keyframing Audio Gain

Getting inside the audio and then plotting keyframe points can be achieved by showing Audio Animation.

1 Apply the audio Gain filter to a clip in the Timeline.

2 Control click the clip to which you have applied the Gain filter and choose Show Audio Animation.

Gain

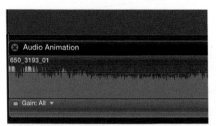

Control-click the Clip and choose Show Audio Animation.

3 A strip is revealed at the base of the audio track. It is here the Keyframe points can be plotted.

Select gain to show Keyframes for relevant to changes in volume

4 Position the Skimmer and press Option Click to mark Keyframe points.

By default further Gain points are added when you move the Playhead and adjust the Gain controls.

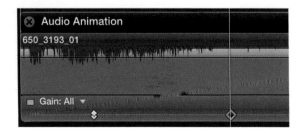

5 Drag the points within the Audio Animation area to raise or lower the gain or make changes to the parameters in the Inspector.

6 To Delete a Keyframe in the Animation Editor click the Audio Keyframe and press the Delete key.

7 Close Audio Animation when you are happy with the result.

Note: The images shown for this section have been for adjusting the audio Gain with Detached audio.

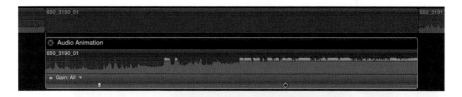

The process with combined video and audio is similar, though be aware that you will be applying Gain changes globally to the stereo or mono tracks. Parameters can be adjusted in the Channel Configuration area of the Inspector.

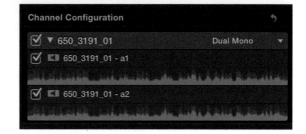

Automated Loudness: Setting Audio Levels Quickly

In general, I'm not a fan of automation, that is, to let Final Cut Pro X take care of tasks which I feel can be better managed manually.

However, there is a fantastic automated control in the Inspector which will boost or reduce the audio level of a clip so that it peaks correctly. You can use this method to sort out the audio levels for individual clips or an entire scene, simply by turning part of the Timeline into a Compound Clip.

1   Highlight the media you wish to work with.

2   Go to the Inspector and select the Audio tab.

3   Choose Audio Enhancements and click the arrow to the right.

Click the arrow to take you into Audio Enhancements.

4   Check the control at the top—Loudness.

The result is that the audio level of the clip is now set to the correct level. You can also adjust Uniformity which affects the overall dynamic range in the audio.

I have used Audio Analysis to enhance audio many times when rushed, to quickly even out audio levels. As written earlier, take a group of several or many clips and turn these into a Compound Clip. Highlight the Compound Clip, go to the Inspector, and then select the audio controls. Click the arrow to the right of Audio Enhancements and check the box for Loudness.

This function works and it works well. However, beware—if music is in the mix some very strange results can occur, so I avoid using this where music is involved. Furthermore, I firmly believe that the best audio mix is the result of human ears listening and interacting to create a result; not the result of pressing a single button to iron out any audio shifts. Thus, I use this method sparingly. But when you're in a hurry and need to get the job done and out the door really quickly, then you do what needs to be done!

Graphic Equalizer

EQing your audio has always been an essential part of the filmmaking process. Sometimes you need to get rid of hiss, other times the audio is too boomy, so the bass needs to be cut.

The Graphic Equalizer in Final Cut Pro X is easy to access and lets you boost and diminish frequencies by dragging and listening. The results play back in real time.

1　Click the clip in the Timeline you wish to adjust.

2　Go to the audio controls in the Inspector.

3　Go to Audio Enhancements and click the Equalization menu to reveal the choices. You can either leave this on flat, which leaves your audio untouched, or you can choose one of the options.

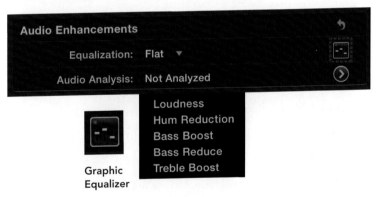

Graphic Equalizer

4　Click the icon to bring up the Graphic Equalizer.

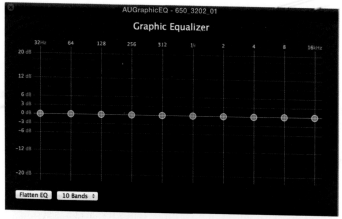

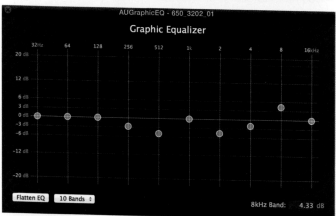

5 Drag the faders to adjust and listen to the result playing back in real time.

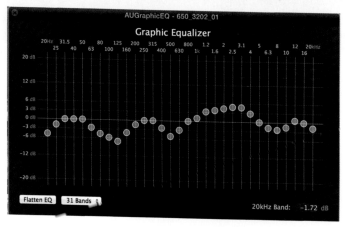

6 For more sophisticated EQing, you can choose a 31-band Graphic Equalizer.

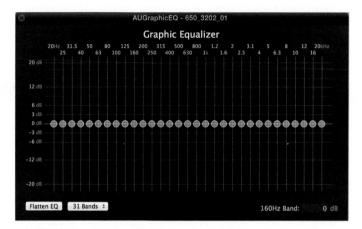

7 You can reset the faders by pressing Flatten EQ.

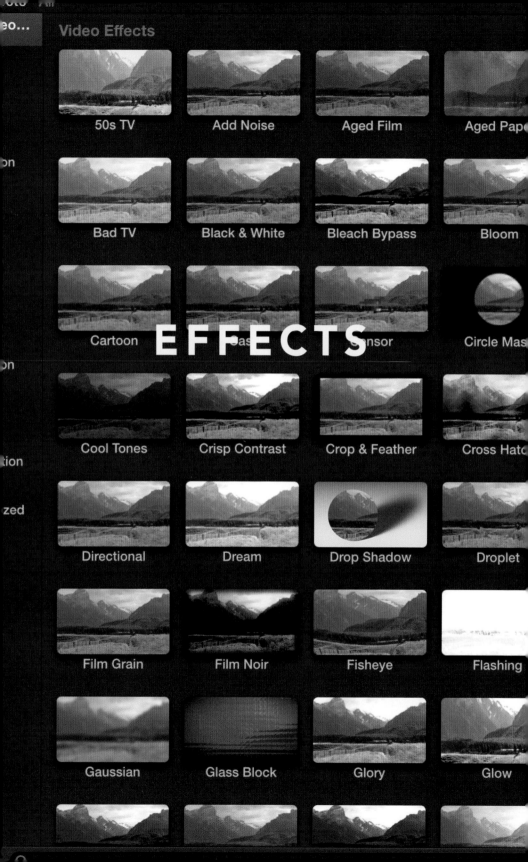

Effects creation is where the action happens. You can combine many elements, composite images, and graphics together, add titles, transitions, and jazz up a production so that it is more than just cuts in a Timeline.

Furthermore, you can treat the images by applying video effects and, if you wish, you have access to a wide variety of prebuilt Templates. Truly remarkable results can be achieved, adjusted, and set according to your needs.

Beyond this is color correction, which offers the ability to sort out white balance issues, tweak the image to warm it up, cool it down, push the black levels, or increase/decrease the whites.

When I started cutting in the late 1980s such power would have been a dream.

Types of Effects

There are five types of effects we are going to be dealing with:

1. Video and audio effects: The effects change the image in terms of color, texture, brightness, and a host of other parameters. Audio too can be manipulated to adjust sound frequencies, level, pitch, and other settings.

2. Transitions: Transitions are applied between clips. The most common transition, the dissolve, is used in all types of productions from home movies to features films. Other wacky transitions can be drawn upon for impact or to add punch to a video.

3 Text: A tremendous amount of text options are offered within Final Cut Pro X for title creation. Everything from a simple static title, to customized moving titles, lower thirds, and captions can be quickly and easily created and positioned.

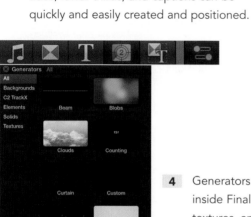

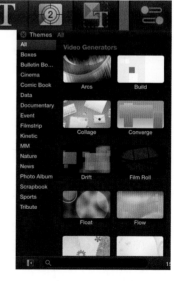

4 Generators: This refers to elements available inside Final Cut Pro X such as backgrounds, textures, and other elements to work with.

5 Themes: Themes are prebuilt moving backgrounds.

Each Theme is divided into two different sections: Video Transitions and Titles.

Themes with text can be customized, which means you can change the color, font, and look of the theme.

The title Themes work as Connected Clips, with the video elements being positioned below the Connected Clip. The video elements are then integrated into the overall graphic.

Transition Themes work between clips and therefore there needs to be existing media on either side of the edit for the Transition to work.

Video and Audio Effects

There is a great selection of effects from which to draw. You can treat your images to create many different looks. Essentially all the effects, video or audio, work in a similar way.

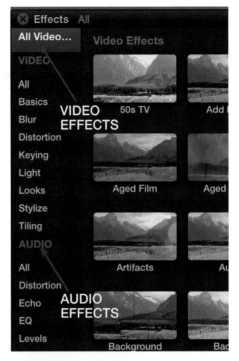

1   Click the Effects Browser icon (shortcut Command + 5). Look at the Effects Browser. There are separate headings for video and audio; click any of the headings to reveal the effects which are available, or choose All to see a complete listing of either video or audio effects.

2   You can preview any of the effects. Click to highlight the clip in the Timeline to which you wish to apply the effect; then position your curser over the effect in the Effects Browser and skim over it. The results will show in the Viewer.

Highlight a clip in the Timeline; select an effect and skim across to preview.

3 With the clip highlighted in the Timeline, double-click the effect of choice. The effect will then be applied. Alternatively, drag the effect from the Effects Browser to a clip and the effect will then be applied. Play it back to view the result.

4 To adjust the effect parameters, select the clip in the Timeline to which the clip has been applied and then look towards the Inspector (Command + 4 to show Inspector).

5 Under Video in the Inspector you will see Effects—here the choices to modify your effect are in front of you. You

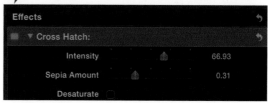

need to be aware that for prebuilt effects, the controls may be limiting. Regardless, there is still a lot that can be done. Experiment, get to know the options, and then you can put these effects to creative use when you need to add some sparkle to a production.

Note: You can easily switch the effect on and off in the Inspector by checking or unchecking the box next to the name of the effect. To remove the effect, click to highlight the effect in the Inspector and press the Delete key.

When working with audio effects, the procedure is the same: Highlight the clip, double-click the effect in the Effects Browser to apply, or use the drag and drop method.

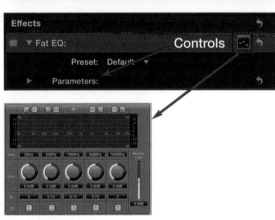

Click the audio of a clip in the Timeline—go to the Inspector and reveal the audio controls. The audio effects are powerful and the results are played back in real time. Therefore, you can adjust video or audio parameters as you play to see or hear the result.

Transitions

Transitions are applied at the edit point between two clips. For a transition to work, you must have media to draw upon from each of the clips on the hard drive, beyond the media which has been edited into the Timeline. For example, for a one second transition to take place, you need half a second of extra media for each clip, to be accessible on drive beyond that which you see in the Timeline.

Media overlaps, also called handles: this enables the transition to take place

1 Press the Transitions Browser icon. You can reveal all of the transitions or view the different categories.

2 Choose a transition and drag and drop. This positions the transition onto an edit point between two clips.

3 View the result. To change the duration, control-click and choose Change Duration.

Alternatively, click to highlight the transition and press Control + D, then enter the duration of choice into the Dashboard and hit Enter.

4 Select a transition in the Timeline. In the Inspector you have controls which will affect the look of the transition. Customize and play back to preview the results.

Note: When adding a dissolve, an audio dissolve will also be applied, if the video and audio are locked together as a single clip. If you have detached audio then a dissolve will only apply to the video.

There are an amazing variety of transitions. Obviously, these need to be used with discretion, so the results are tasteful and appealing. Used well, these transitions can add shine to a production which otherwise may be visually static.

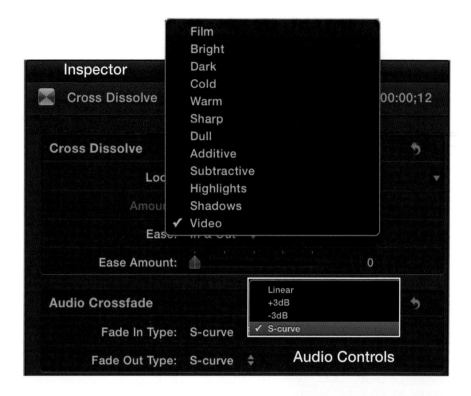

Inspector

Cross Dissolve   00:00;12

Film
Bright
Dark
Cold
Warm
Sharp
Dull
Additive
Subtractive
Highlights
Shadows
✓ Video

Cross Dissolve

Loc

Amou

Eas.

Ease Amount: 0

Linear
+3dB
-3dB
✓ S-curve

Audio Crossfade

Fade In Type: S-curve

Fade Out Type: S-curve   **Audio Controls**

Text

Once upon a time, a simple title would suffice to open a production. These days, moving text, animated text, 3D text, and floating text are the norm—the demand for complex text creation is something that the editor is expected to deliver.

There are a wide variety of text options offered in Final Cut Pro X, ranging from a simple static title to moving text which can be customized in many different ways.

Titles are divided into many different categories.

1 Select the Title icon in the Toolbar to reveal the Title Browser. As with the other effects areas we have looked at so far, you can choose All to see the entire range, or there are separate categories to chose from.

2 Double-click any of the text options and this will be added as a Connected Clip wherever the Skimmer or Playhead is positioned. You can also choose to drag and drop the title from the Title Browser to the position of your choice.

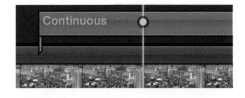

3 In the Timeline, click the title and look to the Inspector. Press Command + 4 to bring the Inspector into view. Look to the top of the Inspector and there are two tabs: Title and Text. You enter text in the Text tab and change parameters in the Title tab.

Here, you can enter the text you wish to work with and adjust parameters such as font, size, spacing, tracking and alignment.

4 Look to the Viewer. Assuming you have clicked the text in the Timeline, the Viewer will display the word "Title" superimposed over the background image.

5 Overtype the text information within the Viewer or in the Inspector window.

6 Adjust attributes of the text in the Inspector.

7 To reposition text in the Viewer, click the icon bottom left, which is a square with circles on the edges. This is referred to as Transform. With Transform enabled you can reposition the text by dragging in the Viewer, resize by dragging the corners towards or away from the center, rotate the text by grabbing the handle in the center, and squeeze the text by choosing the point on the edges of the frame.

Note: The Transform Effect function is not just for titles, it can be used to manipulate video images as well. You can reposition, stretch images vertically or horizontally, and rotate.

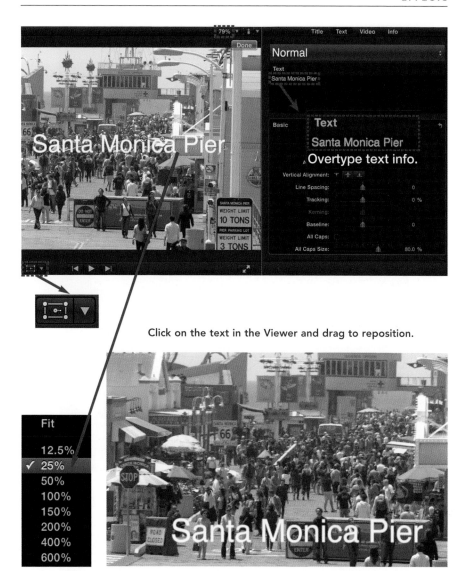

Click on the text in the Viewer and drag to reposition.

Size the image using the percentage values. Choose Fit to make the image use all of the available space in the Viewer, or you can enlarge or reduce the image within the frame. This is simply a visual representation and does not affect the actual size of the image.

Back in the days of film, this required an optical printer and tanks of chemicals to bring the image to life. Now we can make changes and play back in real time. This is a big deal!

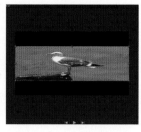

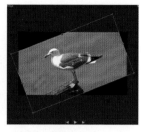

| Increase/decrease size. | Stretch/squeeze the image. | Rotate. |

Creating a Static Title

It is all well and good to have moving, animating, pulsating text, but sometimes you just want the words to sit on the screen, plain and simple.

1 In the Title Browser, select All to reveal all the text options.

2 Locate Custom; you can search for it at the bottom of the Text Browser or scroll down the list until you find it. Apply this to the Timeline by double-clicking or dragging.

3 In the Timeline, click the title, go to the Inspector, and enter the text details in the text area. Choose a font, size, and alignment.

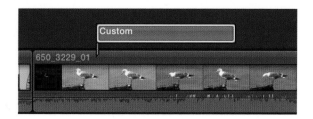

4   You can add color to the text. Check that Face is selected, choose the color, make a choice, and this will be reflected in the words that are on screen. You can also adjust the opacity and the blur.

5   You can also adjust outline, glow, and drop shadow.

Spend some time with text and you can customize the appearance of the words to a high level.

Note: When adjusting fonts you get a long list from which to choose. Each font is represented visually so you can gauge the appearance. If you scroll through the choice of fonts on screen, you will see the words changing so you know exactly how each font will appear.

Going Wacky with Fonts

Whenever you select a title, you have the option to radically change the appearance by drawing on a wide range of pre-built options inside of Final Cut Pro X. The choice is astounding, and the results are impressive. You can also customize the appearance in terms of font, color and many other attributes.

1 Drop a title into the Timeline; double-click it, and look to the Inspector.

2 The top of the Inspector in the text area will read "Normal" in large letters. Choose the drop-down menu to reveal the range of choices.

3 Drag between the choices and choose one of the options. Click and release to see the result.

Click arrows to the right to reveal list of text options.

4 You can now customize the Face, Outline, Glow, and Drop Shadow options.

Fading Titles On and Off and Adjusting Transparency

To fade titles is a basic requirement and this can be achieved quite easily:

1 Choose Custom Title and apply it above a clip in the Timeline.

2 Click the title in the Timeline and refer to the Inspector. Type over the words.

3 Control-click the title in the Timeline. Choose Show Video Animation (shortcut Control + V).

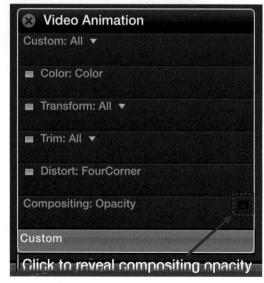

4 The Video Animation window will appear. Click the small arrow to the right of Compositing Opacity. This will open up the opacity controls.

5 Drag the ends to program a fade from the beginning and/or end. As you drag, you can see a numeric representation of the duration of the fade. You can also drag down the

Opacity slider to make the words transparent. As you drag, a percentage read-out indicates the change in opacity.

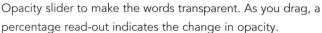
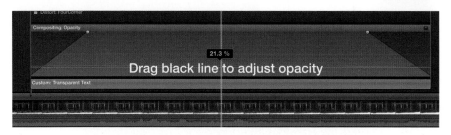

Below: You can see the text is transparent.

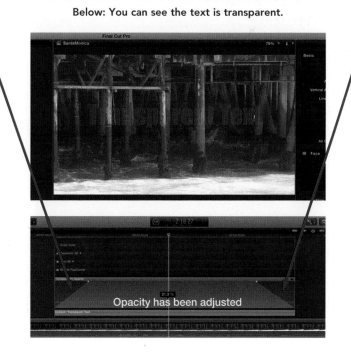

Keyframing Text

So you want to make your text move. You want it to start here and finish there. You wish to program a move so that the text follows a particular path. This can all be done in an elegant way with fine control by keyframing.

1 Place a title into the Timeline—I suggest using Custom Title.

2 Click the text in the Timeline, go to the Inspector or Viewer, and over- type the text as you require.

3 Using the settings in the Inspector, adjust the font, size, tracking, and any other parameters you wish to adjust. You can also adjust the face and add a glow, outline, or drop shadow.

4 In the Timeline, make sure the title is selected; at the bottom left of the Viewer press the Transform Effect icon.

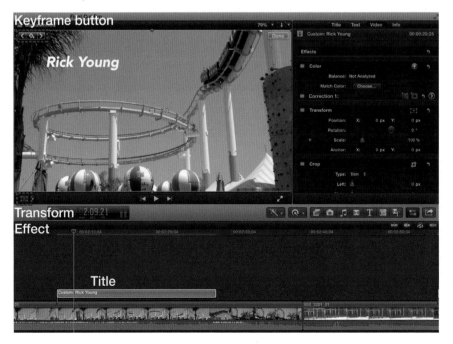

5 You can now freely position the text by dragging. Position and size the text.

6 Position the Playhead in the clip in the Timeline at the location you want the animation (move) to begin. Mark a Keyframe by pressing the Keyframe button at the top left of the Viewer interface.

7 Move forward in the Timeline to where you want the next Keyframe to be added. Reposition the text, rotate it, scale it, whatever you wish to do. This will automatically add the next Keyframe.

Keyframe 1.

Keyframe 2. Note the red line indicating the path of the move.

To see your Keyframes in the Timeline, Control-click the title and choose Show Video Animation (shortcut Shift + V). Look towards Transform All. Here you can see the Keyframes have been plotted.

You can jump Keyframe to Keyframe and forward or backward using the arrows at the top left of the Viewer.

Keyframes can be repositioned by dragging.

8   Control-click the Keyframe points in the Viewer and you can program the move to be smooth or linear.

9   You can choose to lock a point, which means it cannot be dragged; it is fixed.

10   Option-click in the Keyframe editor to add further points. You can add as many Keyframes as you want.

If you Shift + Click the Keyframe points you can then select multiple points at the same time. You can then drag the points, together, in either direction.

Show Title/Action Safe Zones

When working with text, you need to pay attention to the safe area for titles.

When showing video content on a television, as opposed to a computer monitor, you will likely encounter what is known in the industry as cutoff, or the Essential Message Area (EMA). This means that not all of the image is seen on the television screen. As the editor of a program, we need to allow for this.

1. In the Viewer, choose the drop-down menu at the top right, scroll to the bottom, and switch on Show Title/Action Safe Zones.

2. Look to the Viewer. The outer lines represent Action Safe, while the inner lines represent Title Safe.

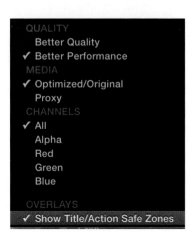

To ensure your titles are seen correctly off-air or on television monitors, position the words within the inside yellow lines.

For content that is not destined for broadcast or television viewing, you can disregard these safe areas; however, it is wise to adhere them, because if your content is shown on televisions then you know it will be safe.

Generators

Generators provide prebuilt media inside of Final Cut Pro X. You can access the generators as a means of creating backgrounds, shapes, or texture to combine within your video compositions.

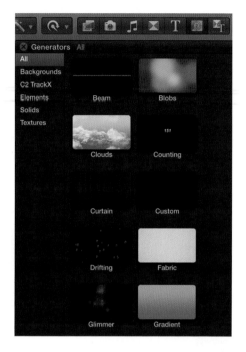

1   Click to reveal the Generators Browser.

2   You can choose to see all the generators which are available, or you can access the various categories.

3   Double-click a generator to add it to the Timeline and it will be inserted wherever the Skimmer or Playhead is positioned. Or you can drag and drop a generator, which can then be added to the Primary Storyline or as a Connected Clip.

Generator inserted into the Primary Storyline.

If you drag a generator between clips it is inserted; if you drag it onto a clip you have the choice to perform a Replace edit.

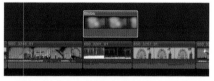

Generator as a Connected Clip.

Replace
Replace from Start
Replace from End
Replace with Retime to Fit
Replace and Add to Audition

Add to Audition

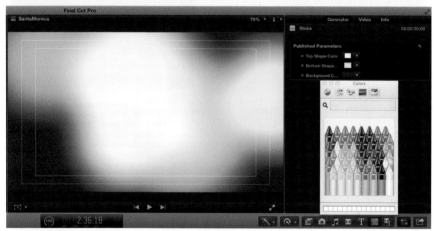

4 You can adjust the parameters of the generator in the Inspector and view changes in real time.

Note: Not all generators allow for adjustments.

Themes

Themes can be either Titles, Generators or Transitions. If a Theme is a Title it works as a Connected Clip; if it is a transition then the theme is applied between two clips; if the Theme is a Generator this can function as a Connected clip or as a clip in the Primary Storyline.

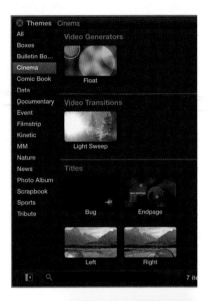

Themes combine graphical elements and text, and sometimes moving images. These are customizable but only to a point. You can change the text size and font, and, in some cases, you will choose moving images which will be integrated into the overall effect.

Working with Title Themes

1 Click to reveal the Themes Browser.

2 You can view all Themes or scan through the various categories.

3 Double-click one of the title Themes or drag into position and this will be added to the Timeline as a Connected Clip.

4 Double-click the title and you can enter text details in the Inspector, or you can type directly into the Viewer. You can also adjust size, font, tracking, and other details.

Other Themes involve prebuilt graphics which include video and text.

The text can be customized in terms of font choice, size, spacing, and color scheme; however, the overall look of the theme and the programmed animation moves cannot be changed.

Working with Transition Themes

As mentioned earlier, Themes can be worked with as either titles or transitions. To work with Transition Themes:

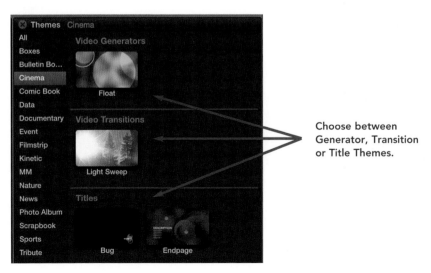

Choose between Generator, Transition or Title Themes.

1   Click to reveal the Themes Browser.

2   Select one of the transition themes; these are clearly labeled as Video Transitions.

3   Drag the Video Transition to the edit point between two clips and this will then be applied.

4   Click the transition to reveal options in the Inspector which can be customized.

Colors can be manipulated and other attributes. These are prebuilt themes. As expected,

the control is limited; regardless, eye-catching results can be achieved by experimenting with the different settings.

5 To set the transition duration, Control-click the Transition in the Timeline, and choose Change Duration (shortcut Control + D).

Control + D and enter duration.

Control-click and select Change Duration.

When working with Themes as Generators, these can be added as either Connected Clips or as a clip in the Primary Storyline. Therefore, the process of working with Generators is essentially the same as either Title or Transition themes, depending on whether the Generator is added to the Primary Storyline, or if it is inserted between two adjacent clips.

Generator Theme added as a Transition.

Generator Theme added as Connected Clip.

Transform Controls

This has already been discussed in-depth in relation to text—the same rules apply to video images when using the Transform Effect Controls. Any shot in the Timeline can be quickly repositioned, resized, rotated, and distorted. Furthermore, changes can be Keyframed over time, meaning the image can be programmed to start in one position and end at another position.

Look to the Viewer—at the bottom is a square with dots in each corner. Click the arrow next to this box to reveal the selection of choices for Transform, Crop and Distort.

Transform

1 Click any clip in the Timeline.

2 Press the Transform Effect button. You will see overlay controls appearing in the Viewer.

3 Click the drop-down menu top right of the Viewer and set the size of the image so it is reduced onscreen.

Fit
12.5%
25%
✓ 50%
100%
150%
200%
400%
600%

Click and drag center point to reposition the image.
Click and drag outer center point to rotate the image.

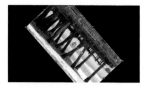

Increase/decrease size.

Stretch/squeeze the image.

Rotate.

4 Drag from any of the corners to increase or decrease the image size.

5   Drag from the center points on the outside frame and you can squeeze or stretch the image.

6   Click the blue dot attached to the center point and you can then rotate the image. If you drag the center point outward, the circle increases in size and this will give you fine control when rotating.

7   Click the center point to reposition the image anywhere inside or outside of the frame.

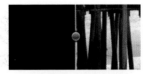

Note: You can also access the Transform Controls in the video area of the Inspector.

Reposition   Rotate

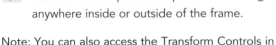

If you wish to Keyframe the video to move over time, the procedure is the same as described earlier in this chapter when keyframing text.

Crop Controls

There are three options offered within the crop controls: Trim, Crop, and Ken Burns.

Trim: to trim the image means to slice away either vertically or horizontally. If the image is positioned over another image, where the image is trimmed will reveal the image below.

Crop: means to select a portion of the image and increase this in size to fill the frame. While sizing, the aspect ratio remains constant; therefore, the area you define is always the correct shape to fill the screen.

Ken Burns: this refers to pan and zoom controls. Named after American film director Ken Burns, who used the effect of panning and zooming across still images—the effect is known for creating moves across still images, but it can just as well be used for moving images.

Trimming Images

1 Highlight the clip in the Timeline.

2 Choose Crop and then select Trim.

Drag edge to Trim.

3 Size the frame around the image by dragging or adjust the Trim controls in the Inspector.

4 Press done.

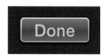

The result is the image shows exactly what you defined. When you trim an image in the Primary Storyline, then the result is black on-screen where you trimmed; if you trim a Connected Clip, where you have trimmed will be filled with the image below the Connected Clip, creating a picture-in-picture, or several picture-in-pictures if you are really creative.

You can also access the controls in the Inspector.

You can also trim by numbers. Highlight the number in the Inspector and overtype, or use the arrow up/down keys for fine adjustment. You can then view subtle changes as you tap the keys.

To reset back to the default, go to the Crop controls in the Inspector and choose the hooked arrow for reset or choose the drop-down menu and select Reset Parameter.

Cropping Images

Adjusting crop is used to
define an area of the
image which will then fill
the screen, whilst
maintaining the original
aspect ratio.

1   Highlight the clip
    you wish to crop in
    the Timeline.

2   Press the Crop
    Effect button on the
    lower left of the
    Viewer Interface.

3   Choose Crop.

4   Drag to set the crop size or use the crop controls
    in the Inspector. You will notice that you are
    constrained to the aspect ratio of the video you
    are working with. You can then position, by
    dragging, the crop area over the image.

5   Press done. The result will be before you—the
    area you defined now fills the screen. Beware of a
    loss of quality by cropping as, essentially, you are
    blowing up the image, or, more precisely,
    cropping in on the image.

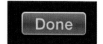

To reset the crop, go to the crop controls in the Inspector and choose the Reset arrow or drop-down menu and select Reset Parameter. You can also adjust the crop controls in the Inspector using the sliders or by entering numeric values.

Working with the Ken Burns Effect

As described earlier, Ken Burns is an American documentarian who made extensive use of panning and zooming over still images. This technique is easy to achieve inside of Final Cut Pro X using the controls provided.

1   Click to select a clip in the Timeline.

2   Click the Crop button in the lower left of the Viewer.

3   Click on the Ken Burns tab bottom center of the Viewer window.

4 Your image will now appear with a green box and a red box—each of these is used to set the start (green) and end (red) points.

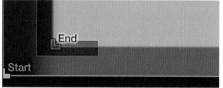

5 Drag the edges of the green box to define the start point of the move. If you want all of the image, leave the green set to the outer edges of the image; if you wish to start already zoomed in to a portion of the image, then frame accordingly with the green box.

6 Drag the red box and size this to define the end of the move. If the red box is smaller than the green box, then you will zoom in to the image. If the red box is larger than

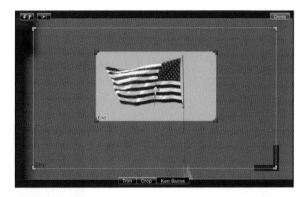

the green box, the result will be a zoom out. Be aware you can also use the crop controls in the Inspector to make adjustments. While adjusting, the aspect ratio will be restricted to that of the frame you are working with.

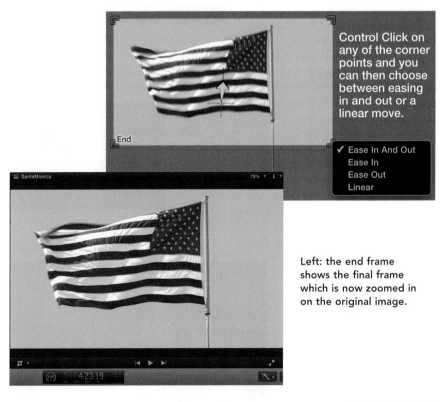

Control Click on any of the corner points and you can then choose between easing in and out or a linear move.

✓ Ease In And Out
Ease In
Ease Out
Linear

Left: the end frame shows the final frame which is now zoomed in on the original image.

7 Press the Done button and press Play to check the result.

You can program beautiful slow zooms or rapid moves in on a portion of the image. Beware with the Ken Burns effect in Final Cut Pro X that the start point is always the beginning of the shot and the end point is the end of the shot. Therefore, if you need greater control, such as having a static image to begin with and then zoom in to, then manual Keyframing would be needed to achieve the result.

Note: You can reverse the start and end points and reverse the direction of the effect. The second button is to play the effect.

To reset at any stage, go to the Crop controls in the Inspector and choose the Hooked Arrow for reset, or, the drop-down menu and then select Reset Parameter.

Distort Controls

Back in the early 1990s, I was watching a demo at a tradeshow on a high-end paint system. The operator was demonstrating a technique known as corner pinning—a digital still was positioned and stretched by dragging each of the four corners. This ability is right there in Final Cut Pro X for you to access.

1   Highlight a clip in the Timeline.

2   Press Distort.

3   Drag the corners and position as you wish. You can choose to crop the image and then distort as you wish.

Using the distort controls enables you to reshape the image by dragging each of the corners.

Above: Two layers composited together with the positioning of the sign done with the distort controls. A tint has been applied to the image on the left.

4 In the Distort Controls of the Inspector, you can key in numbers manually or highlight the numbers and use the arrows to increase or decrease the value.

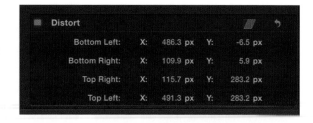

The controls for Transform, Crop, and Distort as found at the bottom left of the viewer are also mirrored in the Inspector. Here, you can manually drag sliders or enter numeric values. If you enter numeric values, highlight the number and use the up/down arrows for subtle changes.

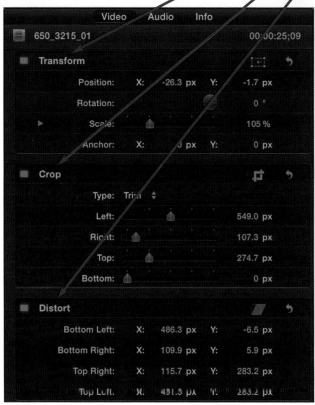

If you Control-click in the Viewer you can choose:

Transform:	Shift + T
Crop:	Shift + C
Distort:	Option + D

Basic Keyframing

Keyframing has already been mentioned several times. It means to change over time.

You can Keyframe text, shapes, and moving images. You can also Keyframe the crop controls such as Transform, Crop, and Distort.

So far we have already covered Keyframing text and Keyframing audio. Let's run through the process for Keyframing video:

1 Highlight a clip in the Timeline.

2 Click the Transform Effect button in the lower left of the Viewer.

3 Position the Playhead in the Timeline on the clip where you want the change to start. Resize and position the clip in the Viewer.

4 Click the Add Keyframe button; this will be your start Keyframe.

5 Move the Playhead forward in the Timeline.

6 Drag to adjust the size or positioning of the image. The next Keyframe will
be marked automatically when you reposition the shot.

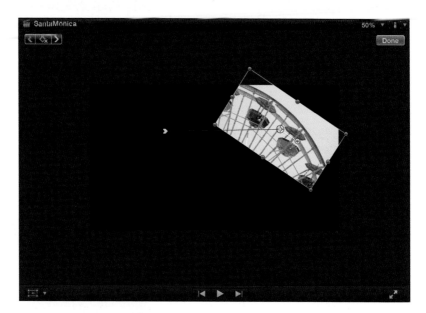

7 You may choose to position the clip you are Keyframing over a second
layer of video (below). Therefore, the two images are composited
together.

8 Play back the content in the Timeline and check the result. If you open the video animation controls (Control +V) and look to Transform All you can then see the Keyframes plotted. These can be dragged to extend or reduce the duration of the effect and further Keyframes can be added by pressing Option + Click in the Transform All area.

New Compound Clip...
Open in Timeline
Change Duration...
Detach Audio
Rename Clip
Disable

Expand Audio / Video
Expand Audio Compone

Show Video Animation

Keyframes plotted in the Transform All area

Click and drag the Keyframes to reposition.

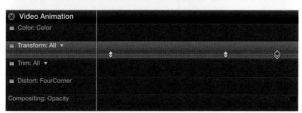

Option + Click to manually add additional Keyframes.

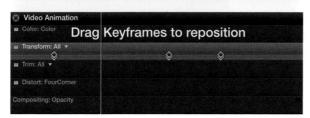

Drag Keyframes to reposition

Shift + Click to select multiple Keyframes and drag to reposition all the Keyframes together.

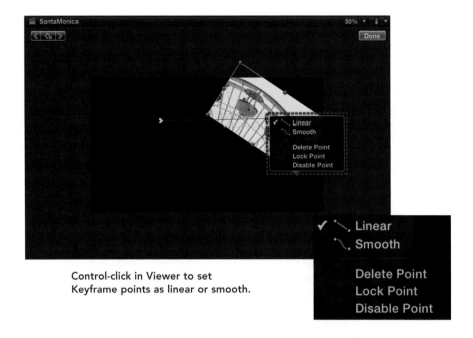

Control-click in Viewer to set
Keyframe points as linear or smooth.

Stabilization

Built into Final Cut Pro X is the ability to add stabilization to any clip. This will remove minor shakes and can dramatically improve the usability of footage.

Simply click the clip in the Timeline, look to the Inspector, and switch on Stabilization (blue).

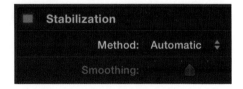

Wait while your footage is analyzed. Once this is done play back to check the results. You can then also switch between the different methods of Stabilization, each of these offer different options on fine-tuning the process. Tripod mode is particularly useful for removing all shake.

Keying

There are two types of keying available, both found in the
Effects Browser of Final Cut Pro X. If you search for "key"
both keyers will be found.

Chroma Key

Chroma Key works on a specific color in the image. Often referred to as blue
screen or green screen, a Chroma Key will be built from two layers: a background
and a keying source. This enables you to key a person, on one layer, over a
background on a separate layer.

The Chroma keyer in Final Cut Pro X is what I refer to as a three-click Chroma keyer.

1 Drop the keyer on the clip in the Timeline.

2 Set key to matte.

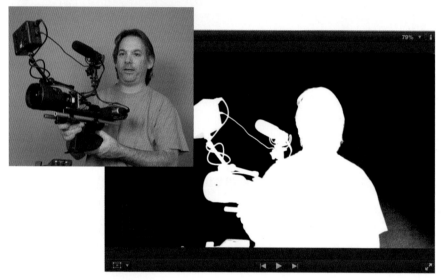

You can see the key is less than perfect. Spill to the bottom right of frame is visible.

3 Refine the key. Go to the Inspector and choose Sample Color. This lets you draw a box over the troublesome area.

Use a matte to check the key is clean and refine the result as needed.

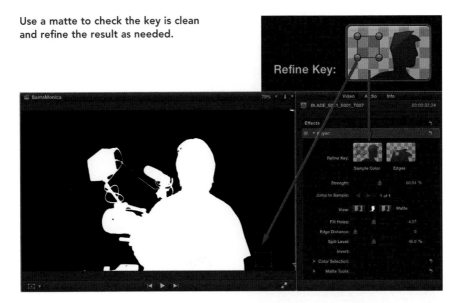

Once you are happy with the key it is then simple to change the background shot to see different results. You can change the background image size, blur the image, add filters, or change the color of the background image.

You can then play back the moving images in real time to check the results. It is therefore possible to create a completely different look with changes that take moments to implement and can then be manipulated however you wish.

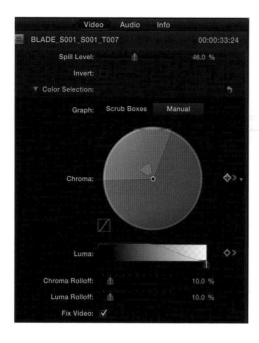

The result can be an excellent key depending on how well shot the camera original is.

You can tweak other settings within the Inspector. From my experience, as long as your original material is well shot and lit you will have no trouble in getting a good key out of Final Cut Pro X.

Having worked with many keyers for over 25 years in this business I can truly say the keyer included with Final Cut Pro X is certainly one of the easiest to use and best of the Chroma keyers on the market.

Luma Key

Luma Key is different to Chroma Key. It works on the amount of luminance in an image, or the difference between black and white. Luma Key used to be used in

television stations to key white word graphics filmed off black card by a live camera over another live source. This example is primitive by today's standards, but shows the history of this technique. Today, Luma Key is used in effects production and image composition.

Luma Keys work particularly well with images that have a lot of contrast or separation of black and white. Look to the image on the previous page. The wire is exclusively black and the other parts of the image are much lighter. This is the sort of image which will key well.

1   Position the two clips in the Timeline with the image to key above the image which is to be the background image.

2   Apply the Luma key to the video source.

3   Select matte so you can check the key level.

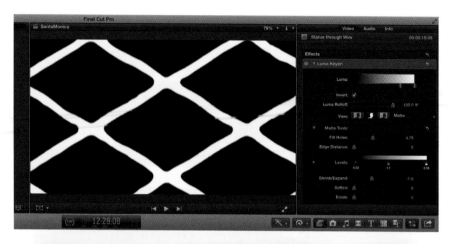

4 In the Inspector tweak the key using the Luma controls. You can invert the source if you wish.

5 Adjust the controls to clean up the key as much as possible.

6 Switch the matte off to view the keyed result and adjust controls in the Inspector as necessary.

Quite effective results can be achieved by Luma keying. The technique is useful for different types of effects production and provides a way to manipulate and composite images.

I've used many Luma keyers and, like the Chroma keyer, the Luma keyer in Final Cut Pro X is definitely one of the best.

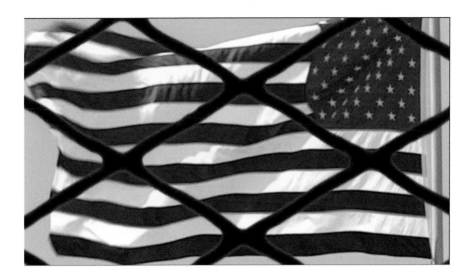

Color Correction

The color correction tools included Final Cut Pro X enable you to achieve results quickly so you can check out a variety of different looks. You can draw on different presets, and you can use dedicated controls to adjust the color, saturation, and exposure of an image. You can also choose to auto-color correct, though this is something which I tend to avoid as the results can be unpredictable.

Check the Balance option and Final Cut Pro X will auto-balance the color for you. As mentioned, I avoid this, as I believe the best results come from manual color correction. Regardless, for a very quick grade, auto-balance is an option.

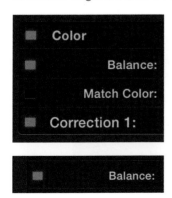

Above: Original.

Above: Auto-balanced.

Now, let's move on to manual color correction.

1 Highlight a clip in the Timeline.

2 Look to the Inspector to the color controls. Make sure auto-balance is switched off.

3 Check color correction is switched on (blue).

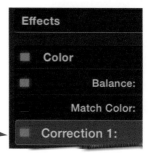

4 Press the arrow to the right of the Correction option and this will reveal three areas for color adjustment: color, saturation and exposure.

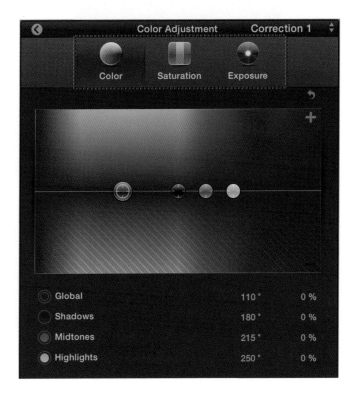

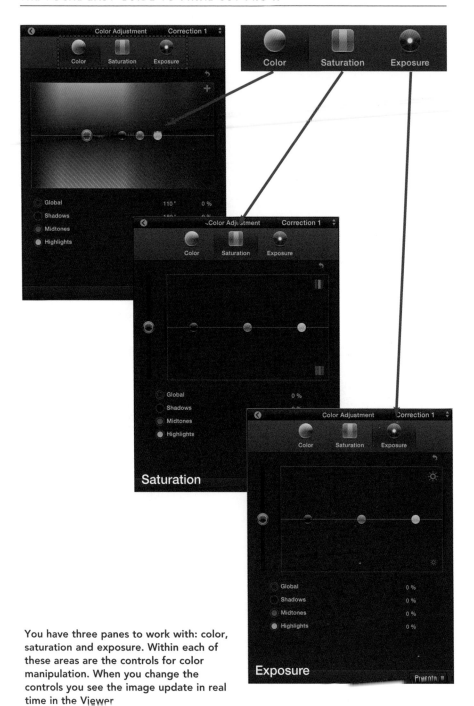

You have three panes to work with: color, saturation and exposure. Within each of these areas are the controls for color manipulation. When you change the controls you see the image update in real time in the Viewer

Color Board

The Color Board is where you make adjustments to the color of the

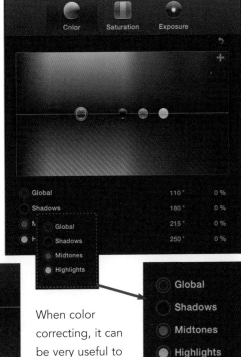

image. You can adjust the color globally, which means change the color across the entire image, or you can choose to be selective about which parts of the image are affected, by choosing to adjust the shadows, midtones, and highlights.

Each of the colors on the Color Board is controlled by the buttons lower left. You choose a button to adjust the image globally, or to target the shadows, midtones or highlights.

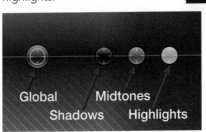

When color correcting, it can be very useful to turn on the video scopes where you can see a waveform monitor or vectorscope display of the image.

Choose the Window menu and scroll down to Show Video Scopes.

The Viewer will now split into two areas: (1) the video scopes and (2) the image you are viewing.

You can quickly toggle the scopes on or off by pressing Command +7.

235

The scopes update in real time as the video plays and you can choose to show a histogram, waveform monitor or vectorscope.

Click settings and choose how you want to view the scopes.

These are professional tools designed to monitor the video signal for broadcast output. If the destination of the content you are producing is for broadcast television, then the scopes are very important. If the content you are producing is to be viewed on computers, home systems, or the web, then you don't need to adhere to broadcast standards. Regardless, this provides a scientific way to monitor the video signal for those who need to do this.

Show Scopes shortcut: Command + 7

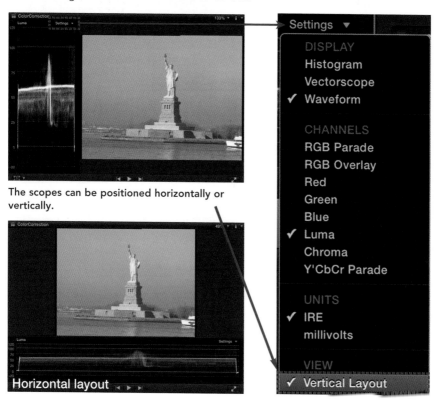

The scopes can be positioned horizontally or vertically.

Horizontal layout

Working with the Color Board

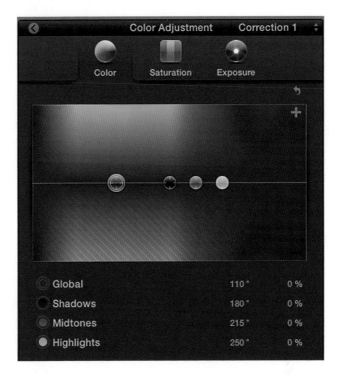

The main job of the Color Board is to enable you to adjust color either globally, meaning throughout the entire image, or to limit the color adjustments to the shadows, midtones or highlight parts of the image.

To adjust the overall color of the image click on the global control and drag it to different parts of the Color Board. The original image is then altered by the color adjustment you make. If you push to the top of the Color Board, the amount of color is increased; if you drop below the middle line and drag in the opposite direction, the amount of color is decreased.

Note: Instead of dragging a control, you can use the up or down arrows on the keyboard for fine adjustment. This also works while video is playing.

The positioning on the color board of the global control directly influences the look of the shot.

Original

To reset to the original, press the Global button so it is highlighted, then press the Delete key.

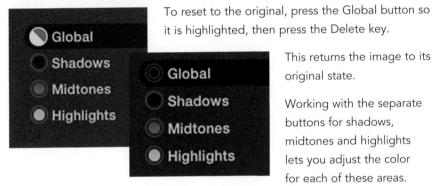

This returns the image to its original state.

Working with the separate buttons for shadows, midtones and highlights lets you adjust the color for each of these areas.

Remember, use the up/down arrows for fine control. This works even while the image plays.

Adjusted

Adjusting Saturation

The process is very similar to that described for working with the Color Board. A master global slider is accessible on the left, with independent controls for shadows, midtones and highlights.

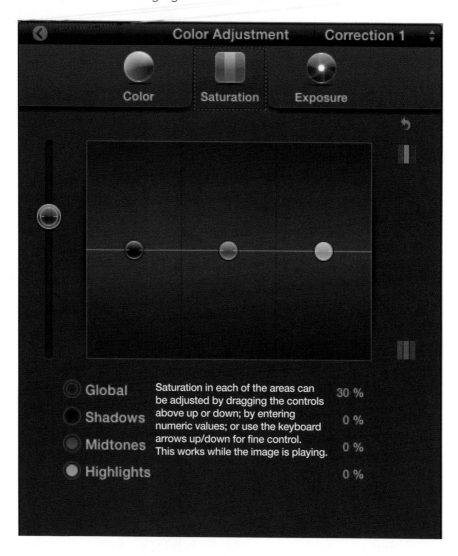

Controls at defaults

Original

Adjust Global, Shadow, Midtones, Highlights

Saturation boosted

Drag the global setting to minus 100% and the result is black and white

Exposure Adjustment

Changing the exposure is an effective tool in bringing out the best in an image. The obvious use is to correct under or overexposed images, and this is a valid use. However, it is not all about getting an image technically correct, it is also about what works best to produce the result you want to achieve. The look of an image can be considerably improved by tweaking the exposure.

The Exposure tools work the same as the process described when adjusting Saturation.

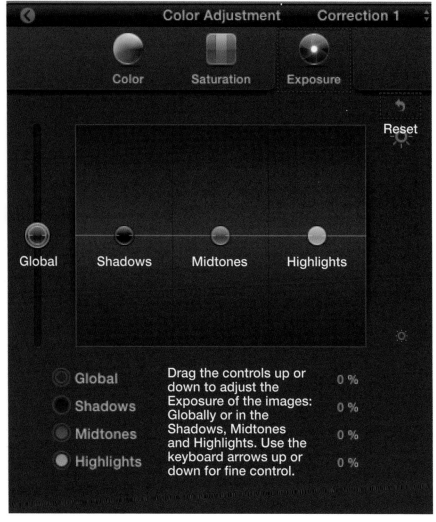

Color Presets

At the bottom right of each window in the Color Adjustment area are presets. You can also create saved custom presets.

Click this and a list will be revealed. These are color presets which can applied to your image. It is as simple as choosing a preset, applying it, and checking out the result.

Save Preset...

Alien Lab
Artificial Light
Ash
Brighten
Cold CCD
Contrast
Cool
Dew
Dim
Dry
Dust
Fall Sun
Frost
Moonlight
Night
Sewer
Spring Sun
Summer Sun
Warm
Winter Sun

Once you have applied the preset you can then go into each of the areas: color, saturation and exposure and change the parameters.

Regardless of which areas you are working in you can reset to defaults by pressing the reset button. You can also highlight any of the circles used to adjust the colors within the color board and press delete, to reset that particular value. This is advantageous over the Reset button which resets all the parameters within a particular area. Think of the Reset button as being a global reset; and highlighting the adjustment circles and pressing Delete as being a more targeted or focused way of doing it.

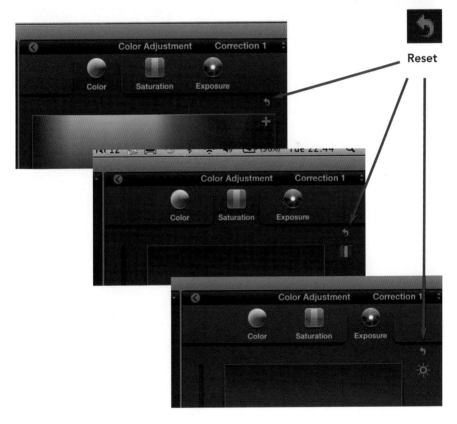

Reset

Once you have manually adjusted the settings, you can save this as a preset:

1   Click the gear icon bottom right
    of the Inspector and choose Save
    Preset.

2   Name the Preset. This will now appear at the bottom of the Preset List.

Original

With preset applied

Save Preset...

Alien Lab
Artificial Light
Ash
Brighten
Cold CCD
Contrast
Cool
Dew
Dim
Dry
Dust
Fall Sun
Frost
Moonlight
Night
Sewer
Spring Sun
Summer Sun
Warm
Winter Sun
Black and White

Paste Attributes

Effects production is a complex area. When you have gone to the effort of setting up all of the parameters of an effect, just as you want it to be, it is then simple to copy all of the settings and to apply these to another clip or to many clips.

This is very useful when you wish to apply the same audio level across many clips, or to position several images to a particular part of the frame. Simply Copy a clip in the Timeline (Command + C) and then choose **Paste Attributes** from the Edit menu. Choose the Attributes you wish to apply and select **Paste**.

1   Highlight a clip in the Timeline with applied Effects and Copy (Command + C). These effects could be a video or audio filter, positioning of an image with the transform, crop or distort

functions, changes to transparency, color correction settings, or many other attributes.

2   Highlight another clip or clips in the Timeline to which you wish to Paste the Attributes to. Select Paste Attributes from the edit menu.

The Paste Attributes window will now open. Notice this window is split into two areas: video and audio. You can therefore choose to apply video or audio attributes, or both.

A visual representation shows the clip from which the attributes have been copied, to the clip to which these attributes will be pasted to.

3   Click Paste, lower right of the Attributes window.

The attributes you highlighted in the window will now be applied to the clip or clips you have selected in the Timeline.

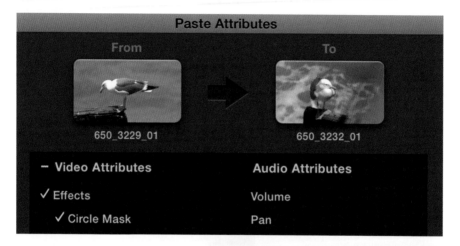

Using Paste Attributes can speed up your workflow as matching exact details can be tedious and time consuming.

In the example of the bird on this page, the attributes of a Circle Mask have been copied and applied to two other clips.

To Paste Attributes from one clip to multiple clips:

1   Copy the Attributes from a clip in the Timeline.

2   Highlight several other clips in the Timeline and then select Paste Attributes.

The result is the original effect is then applied to all the clips you have selected.

There is another command found under the Edit menu which is Copy Effect. This enables you to copy all effect parameters and apply these to another clip without being selective about which attributes are being applied. In other words all attributes will be copied and then pasted.

Share Project

 DVD...

 Master File (default)...

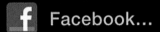 Apple Devices 720p...

 Apple Devices 1080p...

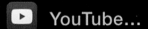 Facebook...

 YouTube...

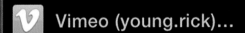 Vimeo (young.rick)...

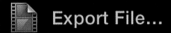 Export File...

Save Current Frame...

Add Destination...

SHARE AND ARCHIVE

Export Media Using Share

When you have finished your movie, the time has come to output. Using the Share facility in Final Cut Pro X you can output to produce a master file, a DVD, Blu-ray, or you can upload direct to YouTube, Facebook or Vimeo. Think of Share as being the output and distribution area within Final Cut Pro X. Share is the final part of the process and enables you to get your edit in front of its intended audience.

By far the most important part of Share, for the professional editor, is the means to create a Master file. This can be created with the same properties as the project, or there are other output settings you can choose from. The

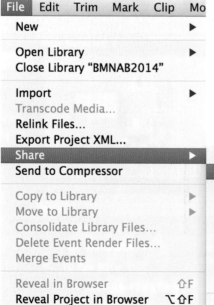

Share command is accessed by pressing the Share icon, located center right of the interface, or Share can be selected from the File Menu.

252

You can export your movie direct from the Timeline—or select the Project in the Browser, and then choose Share.

If you wish to selectively export a section of the Timeline, as opposed to everything in the Timeline/Project, first mark a Range in the Timeline, and then choose Master File.

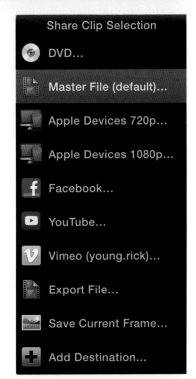

Master File (default)...

Follow the procedure described, making sure you define the codec and destination for the encoded file. The result will be only the area of the Timeline you have defined will be exported.

Note: you can only export a section within the Timeline when working with the Project already open. If you choose to highlight the Project in the Browser, and then select Share, the result will be the entire Project will be exported.

Mark a Range in the Timeline and choose Master File to selectively export an area within the Timeline

On export you can choose to Export Video & Audio, Video only or Audio Only. You can also choose any of the codecs offered in the list of options.

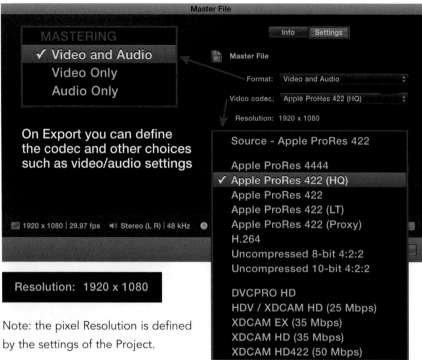

Note: the pixel Resolution is defined by the settings of the Project.

Should you wish to change the resolution this can be done by selecting the Project in the Browser and then, in the Inspector, choose Modify Settings—found in Info.

Modify Settings

Here you can set the project to be anything from 720p to 1080p, 2K,4K, 5K or you can even define a custom size.

Don't be confused by this barrage of information about codecs and image resolution. All we are doing is exporting a file. The technical options simply define the image size, resolution and file type. The video

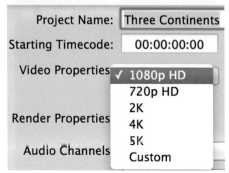

properties applied in Info within the Inspector, will then apply on Export using Share. It is likely that you will seldom need to delve into this area.

In summary, to Export a Master File:

1 Highlight the project you wish to export in the Browser; or, open the Project so the Timeline is open in front of you.

2 Open Share and choose Export Master File.

3 Choose Settings and then choose the codec and define video/audio settings. Much of the time these can be left at the defaults— regardless it is worth checking the settings are as you want them to be before exporting.

Choose settings to reveal the encoding details which you can modify before exporting.

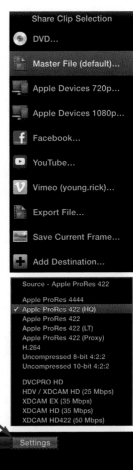

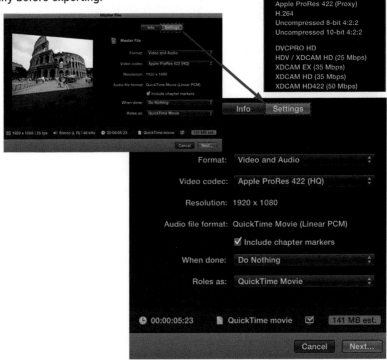

4 Name the file and define the destination where the file will be saved.

Save As: Three Continents

5 Choose Save.   **Save**

To Export a Range within a Project Timeline involves the same procedure, however you need to:

1 Define a Range in the Timeline by marking "i" for in or "o" for out.

2 Choose Share—Master File.

3 Check the codec and other settings are correct, define a destination and Save the file. Once the process is complete an alert will appear to let you know the Share process has been successful.

Save

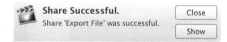

Share Successful.
Share 'Export File' was successful.

Close

Show

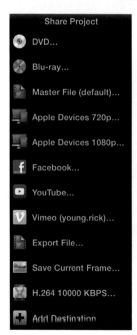

This one command, Create Master file, is crucial to creating a master for distribution and encoding and for creating a secure master of your finished movie.

There are many other export options accessible from within Share.

You can use the Share facility to export to Apple devices, meaning iPad, iPhone, and iPod. The file produced can then be viewed in iTunes on any Mac or on Apple devices.

You can upload to YouTube, Vimeo or Facebook direct from Share.

Of particular use to video editors is the ability to quickly and easily produce a DVD or a Blu-ray of an edit.

Simply choose DVD or Blu-ray from Share and you can then set various parameters to customize the disc. This isn't designed to be a full-blown DVD or Blu-ray authoring system, but it does provide an easy means to produce DVDs or Blu-ray discs for client viewing or other purposes.

For those who use Compressor, Apple's encoding application, you can access Compressor settings from within Share.

Note the Add Destination option at the bottom of Share. This opens the Destinations Preference which enables you to add options to Share beyond the default options.

For example, you can add Export Still, Blue-ray, Custom Compressor settings, Image Sequence, Save Current Frame and other settings.

Choose the option within the Destinations window, drag this into the list of Destinations and release your mouse. You can then reorder items within

Destinations as you wish. Furthermore, highlight an item and use the minus (−) control to remove items from the list.

Once you have made your changes, close the Destinations window and then open Share, and the changes you made are then reflected in the list of Export Options.

When you select an export option from Share you will be presented with choices in Settings. For example, to upload to Vimeo you need to enter account information; to create a DVD or Blu-ray you may wish to define a background image for the menu; to Save Current Frame allows you to save a still as a JPG, TIFF, PDF or PNG file.

Share gives the means to export your digital movie, or a portion of your digital movie; to create a high quality master; to encode the movie to different codecs; and to upload the movie for online digital distribution.

The key to getting effective results from Share is to check the Settings.

For example, you may choose to export a Still using Save Current Frame. Go into Settings, check the options, define the file type, then choose a location on drive to save the Still.

Choose the file type for the still you are to export.

You may wish to build a DVD. Choose the
DVD option from Share; select Settings
and look at the options. You can define a
still for the menu background, decide
when the disc loads to Show Menu rather
than to Play Movie straight away, plus
there are other choices to consider.

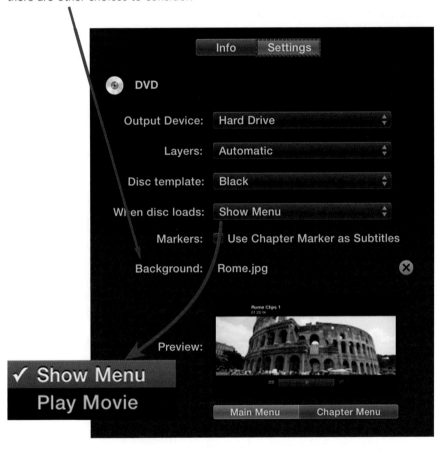

The choices you make directly affect the output result, so take the time to
explore these areas. If you are unsure about encoding options or some of the
choices presented, then experiment! This is how you will learn. Most of my
encoding knowledge has come from direct experience of seeing what works best
in terms of quality versus file size.

Media Management

Media management is something which happens when you set up your project, during importing media, and throughout the entire editing process. If done correctly, when you get to the end of the project, providing your media has been managed correctly, there isn't a great to deal to do other than the very important task of effectively archiving the Library and all the Projects within it (dealt with next!)

In terms of Media Management there are a few tips to help you along the way.

Delete Render Files for Projects and Events

If you have Background Rendering switched on in Preferences—or if you choose to manually render while working, inevitably this will generate render files which will, at some point, no longer be needed. Furthermore, even Render files which are needed can easily be generated again if you choose to clear these from drive.

To delete render files from an Event:

1 Highlight the Event.

2 Choose the File Menu and scroll to Delete Generated Project Files. You will then be presented with a window presenting you with choices to Delete Render Files, or to Delete Optimized Media or you can Delete Proxy Media. Choose carefully! While the media can be regenerated this does take time.

3 Make your selection of which files you wish to delete and click OK.

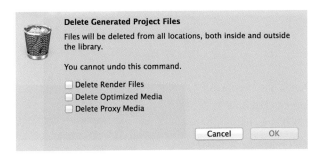

To delete render files from a single or multiple Projects:

1 Highlight the Project or Projects in the Browser which you wish to delete the render files from.

2 Choose File—Delete Generated Event Files.

3 A window will open providing you with options—choose Delete Render Files.

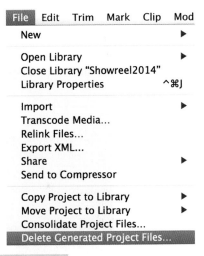

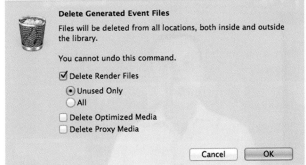

4 With Delete Render Files selected—then decide if you wish to Delete Unused Only or All the Render Files on hard drive.

The main reason to render content in the Timeline is for smooth playback of video at full resolution. The main reason to delete render files is to free up hard drive space.

Relink Media

Sometimes Final Cut Pro X and the media in the Browser and/or Timeline can become disconnected. This is usually due to human error, when files are copied, moved or deleted from hard drive. When the link is broken between Final Cut Pro X and the project media, a yellow warning will appear in each of the Event headings, and red icons will indicate missing files in the Browser and also the Timeline.

Both the yellow triangle and red icons indicate missing files.

The solution to the missing files is to Relink to the media. Once this is done the red offline warnings in the clips will disappear and the yellow triangle in the Event titles. You can then access the media.

Above: Missing files in Icon View in the Browser.

Above: Missing files in List View in the Browser.

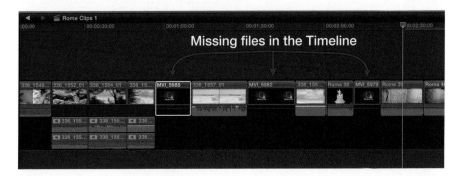

Above: Missing files in the Timeline.

To relink to media requires you to know where that media is. The Relink command enables you to relink to media, however, it doesn't find the media for you.

The easiest way to locate media is to do a Search for it. Look at the clip names on the missing media—you can even click on the name of a missing clip within an event, highlight this and copy the information. Then click on the Mac Desktop—or select Finder from the dock, invoke the Apple Search Facility (Command + F) and enter the information of the missing media. Once you have located this—then you can relink to it. If you highlight several or many clips you can then relink to media in bulk.

1 Highlight the Missing Files which you wish to relink to.

2 At the top of the Final Cut Pro X interface choose the menu File— Relink Files.

3 A window will open giving you the option to Relink to Missing Files or All Files. I suggest relinking only to Missing Files

4   Press the Locate All button.

5   Navigate to the folder on hard drive which contains the missing files. Click Choose to select from the folder.

6   Press the Relink Files button to Relink the missing media.

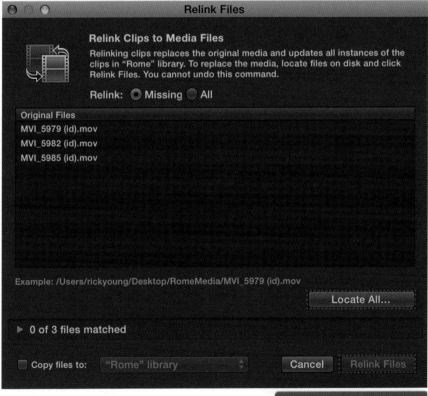

Once relinked, the yellow and red warning will disappear and the media is available for you to work with.

Archive and Backup

Archive or Backing Up of your entire Library is very different to creating a Master File. On one level, creating a Master File is archiving the edited movie, however there are times when we need more than this.

In addition to needing the edited movie archived, we also need the entire Library and all the Projects contained within the Library to be backed up and archived— so at any time we can return to the master edit and change this, re-edit it as necessary, perhaps create foreign language versions, promos, shorter or longer versions . . . Essentially, we must be able to return to the master edit at any time, and we also must protect the edit! Which means storing all of the content on at least 2 hard drives.

Archiving of your entire Library and all of the Projects, media, proxy files, and anything else within the Library, is delightfully simple.

You simply copy the Library from one hard drive to another.

Let me repeat that—**You simply copy the Library from one hard drive to another.**

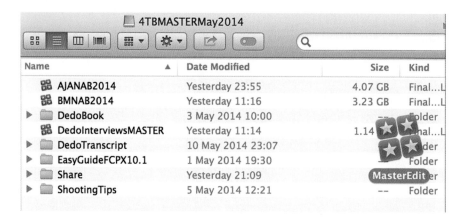

Make sure that the hard drive you are copying to is large enough to contain the Library being copied and all media associated with it!

Once the process of copying the Library from drive to drive is complete, you need to select the command Consolidate Media from the File Menu in Final Cut Pro X.

Once the Consolidate Media command has been selected, any media which is external to the Library you are working with will then be copied into this Library. The result is all media within the Library is internal—nothing is external!

This is the key to successful archiving. Let me repeat the fundamental steps:

1 Copy the Library you wish to archive from one drive to another.

2 Once the copy process has taken place, open Final Cut Pro X. Highlight the Library in the Browser and choose File—Consolidate Library Files.

3 You can choose to include Optimized Media and Proxy Media. Click OK and the media will then be written to hard drive within the Library you have chosen to consolidate.

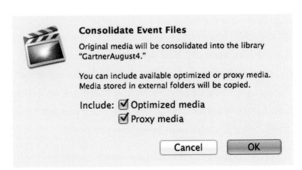

Let the process Consolidate Library Files take place. This may take some time if there is a lot of media to copy.

A Consolidated Library can get quite large, particularly if there are many different Projects with hours upon hours of media within the Library.

If you try to consolidate a Library which already has all media internal, then there will be nothing to consolidate. You will get a message to let you know that the files already exist in the selected location.

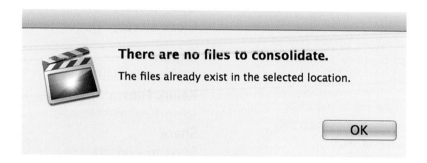

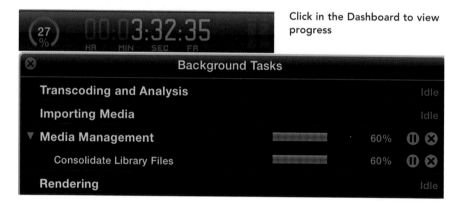

Click in the Dashboard to view progress

Once the Consolidate Media process is complete, I then quit Final Cut Pro X, disconnect all hard drives from the Mac and restart. I then connect up the drive with the copied Library, which now has had the media consolidated into the single Library. I then open this Library. Providing there are no yellow triangles or red missing media symbols within any of the Events or project timelines, then you know that the Library is intact with everything in place.

You now have a master backup of the Library with Projects and Media. You can then choose to back this up to a third hard drive, or solid state solution such as Blu-ray, or a long-term tape archive solution such as LTO.

Do not underestimate the importance of this final archiving stage, as doing this will protect the Projects, the Library and all of the master media so you can return at any stage for further postproduction work.

Note: when you click on a Library in the Browser, you are then presented with some important choices within the Inspector. In the image below you can see that you can Modify Settings or you can Consolidate Media.

Choosing to Consolidate opens the same window and gives you the same choices which you are given when choosing the command Consolidate Library Files from the File menu.

If you choose Modify Setting you can then define: where media files will be stored—you can choose somewhere other than the Library; you can choose where Cache files will be stored; and very important, you can also choose where the Backups will be located.

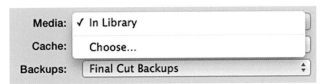

While you can well and truly leave these settings at their defaults, it can be advantageous to manually define these Storage Locations. Before you start messing about too much, make sure you know what you're doing and exactly where your media will be stored.

ENJOY
THE RIDE

◀ ▶ ▶|

We're living in a digital age in which the moving image and the ability to create moving images are now as common as the still image. Just about everyone has a video camera of some sort, whether it is in a camera phone, a dedicated video camera or some other device. Video literacy is the foundation of mass media in the twenty-first century and being literate in producing edited content is found from schoolchildren to professional editors.

Whether you edit at the professional level or for other reasons, Final Cut Pro X provides the means to produce content exceptionally quickly with top-level results. The tools are there to draw on, it depends how good you are, as the editor, to pull it all together and really make it work.

I started editing on a Mac way back in 1998. Before then I was working in tape suites. I've been exposed to many systems from film editing to multi-machine tape editing, the original Final Cut Pro and many other computer-based editing systems.

Final Cut Pro X is different. The approach is different to many of the other editors on the market. The benefits are clear if you can absorb this way of working and refine it to your own needs.

In this book, I have outlined many of the work methods I use to get results using Final Cut Pro X. I'm a professional editor; I produce content daily and weekly for paying clients. I use Final Cut Pro X because it works for me, and more importantly, it produces results my clients are happy with.

When Final Cut Pro X was released in June 2011, amid a firestorm of controversy, I said to someone at the time: "Can it do a cut? Can it do a dissolve? Can it separate audio from video?" The answer was obviously yes! "So what's the problem?" was my reply.

That's it! Go and edit. The way to learn Final Cut Pro X is to use it. The tool is good, now make it work, so you hit the mark, dead center, bull's eye, every time.

Index

Page numbers in **bold** refer to figures.

Bound to Create

You are a creator.

Whatever your form of expression — photography, filmmaking, animation, games, audio, media communication, web design, or theatre — you simply want to create without limitation. Bound by nothing except your own creativity and determination.

Focal Press can help.

For over 75 years Focal has published books that support your creative goals. Our founder, Andor Kraszna-Krausz, established Focal in 1938 so you could have access to leading-edge expert knowledge, techniques, and tools that allow you to create without constraint. We strive to create exceptional, engaging, and practical content that helps you master your passion.

Focal Press and you.

Bound to create.

> We'd love to hear how we've helped
> you create. Share your experience:
> **www.focalpress.com/boundtocreate**

 Focal Press
Taylor & Francis Group